The Horse
of My Heart

Other books by Callie Smith Grant

The Cat on My Lap
The Dog at My Feet
The Cat in the Window
The Dog Next Door

The Horse of My Heart

Stories of the Horses We Love

Edited by

Callie Smith Grant

Revell

a division of Baker Publishing Group
Grand Rapids, Michigan

© 2015 by Baker Publishing Group

Published by Revell
a division of Baker Publishing Group
P.O. Box 6287, Grand Rapids, MI 49516-6287
www.revellbooks.com

Printed in the United States of America

Library of Congress Cataloging-in-Publication Data
The horse of my heart : stories of the horses we love / edited by Callie Smith Grant.
    pages cm
    Includes bibliographical references.
    ISBN 978-0-8007-2334-7 (pbk.)
    1. Horses—Anecdotes. 2. Human-animal relationships. I. Grant, Callie
Smith.
    SF301.H643 2015
    636.1—dc23   2015015865

16 17 18 19 20 21 22   9 8 7 6 5 4 3

Contents

Contents

Contents

Introduction

Callie Smith Grant

As a younger adult I moved around for my work, and for a couple of years, I lived in New York City. While there, I participated in a writers' group where every member was a native New Yorker except me. I was the lone country girl.

The advice of the day to young writers was, *Write what you know*. So I often wrote about growing up in the country. One day I brought to the group a story about feeding the horses on dark winter mornings. The other writers liked the piece, but they were surprised by it. "Where are the adults in this story?" one asked. "Why are children handling those huge animals with no adults around?"

That's hard to answer if people aren't familiar with horses. The fact that horses are large is not the whole story. Anyone who has had horses or worked around them knows they are potentially dangerous, yes. But horses are complicated. They are prey animals who look to their humans—even human children—for care and safety. I remember as a child being very aware that these big beasts trusted me and did my bidding, and I was amazed by it. The fact that we ride horses means we have a very different relationship with these herd animals than we have with a house pet.

Fully exploring the human-horse relationship is beyond what I can do. I'll let the contributing writers tell those stories. There are stories here from both men and women, and I learned that more women than I ever imagined wanted horses when they were girls. (Raise your hand if you collected Breyer model horses!)

These remarkable stories run the gamut from the intimate friendships between human and horse to seeing a horse as a metaphor for some aspect of one's life. Some horses in these stories show up at the right time—to help a healing man gain strength, help a woman move on after grief, help a young man feel capable, even help people in hospitals. Horses aid a child with anxiety or another child who won't speak. Some horses provide an opportunity to learn something new—how to handle bullies, how not to judge by appearance, how to trust.

Sometimes the horse's strong, steady presence helps people adjust to life changes or helps a teenager stumble through adolescence. Sometimes the helping is mutual—rescue the horse and the horse rescues you back. In a few stories, the horse is background or a symbol for a whole other experience. And you'll meet another equine—a sweet-natured donkey whose surprise appearance helps a family laugh through the tough times.

I hope you enjoy these stories as much as I've enjoyed collecting them. Now let's join the storytellers in this book and have a closer look at some of the most magnificent animals in creation.

The Pasture Bully

Susy Flory

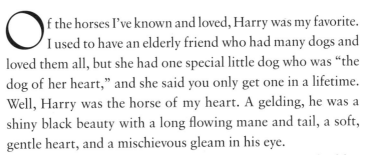

Of the horses I've known and loved, Harry was my favorite. I used to have an elderly friend who had many dogs and loved them all, but she had one special little dog who was "the dog of her heart," and she said you only get one in a lifetime. Well, Harry was the horse of my heart. A gelding, he was a shiny black beauty with a long flowing mane and tail, a soft, gentle heart, and a mischievous gleam in his eye.

Whenever Harry heard me approach, he always tilted his head, then bobbed it up and down with a friendly nicker, eyes bright. He was easy to catch but not easy to keep tied to the hitching post—he was a master at untying the knots in the lead rope when you weren't looking and then wandering away to snatch a few mouthfuls of grass. When I caught up, he always looked innocent. "Who, me?" You'd almost believe it was an accident if you didn't see the twinkle in his eye.

Even though he was mischievous, Harry got along well with the other horses, including the pasture bully, a big-boned white Appaloosa with a smattering of tiny, red spots. Her name was Mesa, and she had a first-class bad attitude. Mesa was quick to lay her ears flat against her head and fix an angry glare at whoever was blocking her way to the feed box, the water trough, or her preferred patch of grass. The other horses knew to stay out of her way when she wanted something, because she wasn't above striking out with a back hoof or baring her teeth and biting whoever was in the way. The other horses just let her do whatever she wanted.

Harry finessed the situation, though. He avoided her when she was on the rampage and waited until she was otherwise occupied to sneak in and grab some hay for himself. He never confronted Mesa head-on. Harry was too smart for that.

One day, when I was about ten years old, my dad told me the best news ever—our quarter horse mare had just given birth to a beautiful foal. Dad, my sister, and I raced to the stable and quietly watched the new baby nestled in the straw, her proud mama licking and nudging her. We immediately named her Honey to match her rich, red-gold coat and watched through a window into the stall as Honey stretched her legs and awkwardly tried to stand. Foals are all legs, and those long spindly legs seem to bend in all directions when they're first born. Honey tried to stand, then collapsed, then tried again. Eventually her legs worked, and she got her first taste of warm milk, her curly tail wiggling in delight.

Every day after school, I hurriedly grabbed my backpack to race home to see Honey. But most afternoons I faced my own bully. One of the boys in my class used to hide behind a fence and wait for me, then jump in front of me and kick me in the shins before laughing and running away. I was tall for my age, but he was taller. I tried to outrun him, but he'd just run after me and give me a shove. I didn't know what to do, so I took the kicks, then ran home.

Honey was curious and quickly grew tame, allowing me to stroke her neck and back while she leaned against me, snuggling into my side. But within a month the snuggling was over, and Honey was scampering around the stall, jumping and playing and driving her poor mama crazy. My dad decided it was time to let the pair out into the pasture, where mother and daughter could stretch their legs.

On the appointed day, Harry, Mesa, and the other horses were up high on the hill, grazing peacefully in the spring sunshine when Dad released Honey and her mother into the pasture. Honey stayed close by her mom, and they slowly wandered across the base of the hill. We watched as the rest of the horses looked up, watched the release, then went back to grazing. Horses came and went from the pasture all the time, so the herd didn't pay much attention, especially if there was no hay involved.

We had just turned to leave when we heard a loud neigh, then a squeal. "Dad, what is that?" I yelled. We ran back to the gate and tried to see what was going on. *Mesa!* We looked in horror as Mesa, now at the bottom of the hill, ran back and forth in front of mother and baby, stirring up dust and screeching. When a horse screeches, it's never good news. Mesa's legs were stiff as she charged back and forth, her tail stuck out at an odd angle like a battle flag. Her ears were back and she made sharp, jabbing motions with her head. She wasn't yet within striking distance, but she was close.

Honey, clearly terrified, was hiding behind her mom, who trotted nervously back and forth, mirroring Mesa's movements.

My dad rushed over to the fence and waved his arms, trying to scare Mesa off. "Mesa, get out of here. NOW!" he shouted.

The mare wheeled around, angrily flipped her tail, and ran back up the hill. Honey and her mom also took off running along the fence line at the bottom of the hill away from us. My sister and I started crying, sure that our precious baby foal was going to die at the angry hooves and teeth of the massive spotted horse. Dad rushed back toward us and opened the gate while we screamed, "Daddy! Daddy! Please help Honey!"

At the top of the hill, Mesa trotted around, back and forth, then headed down toward the right. She still looked like she was on the warpath. Then it happened. The other horses, who'd been staying out of the fray at the top of the hill near the trees, parted, and out trotted Harry. He crossed over in front of Mesa but never once looked at her. He slowed to a walk, then headed purposefully down the hill to the right. My dad saw the black figure moving toward Honey and her mama and stopped to watch at the gate.

Harry's body language was calm and collected. His ears were up and forward, his body relaxed and moving gracefully, and he looked like he was just a gentleman out for a Sunday afternoon stroll. When he was about twenty feet away, he stopped, looked at Honey and her mother, then dropped his head and began to sniff the grass. He moved a few feet, sniffed again, and began to nibble.

Honey's mother looked at Harry grazing and copied him, dropping her head and beginning to nibble at the grass too. Honey stayed close by her side.

Then Mesa was on the move again, walking in ragged, agitated circles at the top of the hill. The circles grew larger and larger, and pretty soon she broke her pattern and came down again, circling in from the left and heading toward Honey. Her ears went flat against her skull, and her front legs pounded the ground as she walked.

What is wrong with her? Why does she want to hurt Honey? It didn't make any sense. Honey was no threat. Neither was her mother. The truth is, Mesa was just a bully, and she wanted to be the boss. Usually her aggressive behavior worked and she got what she wanted, when she wanted. But this time was different.

When Mesa approached, Harry stopped eating. He lifted his head and turned to watch Mesa. When she was about forty feet away, he turned his whole body to face her and grew very still, mama and foal behind watching nervously. Mesa veered to the left, still walking. Harry moved again to face her. Mesa stopped, looking at Harry. He regarded her calmly. She started walking again and veered to the right. So did Harry. Then Mesa stopped, looked at Harry, and dropped her head, nibbling at the grass. Harry watched her for a minute, then did the same. Harry stayed put, with Mesa in front and Honey and her mother behind him.

Mesa's body language changed when she realized Harry wasn't going to back down. I couldn't believe it as her ears went back up, her body relaxed, and she turned around and grazed her way back up the hill. I watched, relieved, and knew that dear, sweet Harry had thwarted Mesa's bloodlust and saved Honey's life. My dad quickly went into the pasture, gathered up Honey and her mom, and led the pair out and back to their stall. Harry watched, and when the gate shut behind mom and baby, he wandered back up the hill and rejoined the herd.

A few days later, Dad let Honey and her mother out in the pasture, and once again Harry put himself in front of Honey and her mom and stayed there, like a bodyguard. Mesa approached aggressively, but Harry stood his ground, and she soon gave up. For the next few months, that's how it went. Mama and baby relaxed, enjoying the sweet grass, while Harry guarded them and kept the peace.

After watching what Harry did that first day, the very next day I decided to confront my own pasture bully. When the mean boy ran out from behind the fence after school, I looked him in the eye and said calmly, quietly, "You *stop* it. Leave me alone. If you kick me ever again, I'm going to tell your mom!"

And you know what? He never did kick me again. I don't think it was the threat to tell his mother that worked. Instead, it was the power of standing my ground. Harry taught me that sometimes you just have to face the bully head-on. And when you do, he might just turn tail and walk away.

Police on Horseback

You've most likely heard of the Royal Canadian Mounted Police. But cities all over the world have divisions of police on horses. There are proven reasons for cities to have mounted police. On good days, they are animal ambassadors to the population. And of course they look handsome in celebrations. On tenser days, they work well with crowd control, and the general rule in those situations is that one mounted police officer equals twelve police officers on foot.[1]

Scooter

Katy Pistole

M y eyes scanned the want ads of the local paper. I had
recently lost my beloved Arabian, Beau, to inoperable
colic, and I was looking for another horse. I was not looking for
a rescue or a project. My heart ached too much for that kind of
emotional outflow. I finally saw an ad that sounded promising:

*Three-year-old, fifteen-hand, chestnut Arabian, green-broke,
leads, loads, stands for the farrier.*

Perfect. I called and spoke to a man I'll call "Joe" because I
don't remember his real name. I told Joe my sob story about
losing Beau. He told me I'd better bring my trailer and arrive
early because other folks were interested in his horse.

I arrived at the "farm" early the next morning with $500 in
my pocket. It was all I had to spend, so I hoped Joe would be
willing to negotiate. The farm consisted of a dilapidated barn
surrounded by a saggy barbed wire fence. Old cars and rolls of
rusty barbed wire littered the large field to the right of the barn.

I parked my truck and trailer, climbed out, and scanned the horizon, looking around for any signs of equines. Joe emerged from the barn, lugging two buckets of sweet feed, a lead rope over his shoulder. He handed me a bucket, and we headed toward a rusty gate.

Joe whistled, and a small herd of horses, mostly black draft horses, appeared from over a hill and thundered down upon us.

"Quick!" Joe yelled. "Make some piles of grain! And spread 'em out!" He ran ahead, dumped his bucket in three or four places, and stood back. I did the same.

The drafts found the grain and started munching. A little chestnut horse—no more than 14 hands—followed the draft horses and approached a pile of grain cautiously. The horse's hindquarters were covered in strange cuts, each about five inches long. It looked as though he'd had a run-in with some barbed wire. I shook my head. I hate barbed wire.

Joe sidled over and made a grab for the halter. The little horse scooted just out of reach. Joe, clearly familiar with this scenario, had saved some grain and held the bucket in his outstretched arms, inviting the red horse to eat. "Come on."

The horse craned his neck, reaching, reaching, reaching, while Joe slowly brought the bucket closer to his chest. Finally the horse had to take a step forward, and immediately Joe grabbed the halter and clipped the lead rope. The horse reared and Joe held tight. As soon as the gelding's front feet hit the ground, Joe handed the rope to me. I watched the little red horse plunging at the end of my line and asked the whereabouts of the horse I'd come to see.

Joe cocked his head and pointed at the airborne Arabian. "That's him."

I sighed. I must be wearing a big S for sucker.

But I knew I could not leave the little horse where he was. I protested weakly, "I'm not sure he's quite what I'm looking for."

Joe's eyes glistened and his shoulders drooped. "You've got to take him. I'm doing things I shouldn't. He just makes me so mad!"

Suddenly I knew the strange cuts were from a whip. And my mind was made up.

"I've got $500. Will you take that?"

Joe stared at his boots for a moment. "I paid a lot more for him . . . I really do love him. I can't handle him."

I'd bought myself a project. It took fifteen minutes to load him into the trailer, and Joe was amazed.

"Didn't think you'd get him in so fast."

So much for "leads, loads, stands for the farrier."

Joe gave me the horse's registration papers, and I glanced at his name. I had to smile. There was no way I would call him that. On the way home I thought about a new name.

Scooter. It fit. He entered the trailer with one name; he would emerge with a new name.

Now *my* work would begin.

There are some hurdles in rescuing horses. A significant hurdle is that horses are prey animals. That means they provide meat for predators. And humans are predators. This makes us enemies by nature. Prey animals do not naturally cooperate with predators. Another hurdle in rescuing abused horses is their psychology. They think in patterns. That means, in Scooter's mind, all humans would beat him. The third and largest hurdle in rescuing horses is their language. Horses, like many prey animals, are mostly silent. They communicate with each other using rhythm and pressure. And horses are incredibly perceptive. Humans, not so much.

I had to be perceptive and aware of Scooter's body language and my own. I would need to prove to Scooter that I was different from Joe. I wanted him to know he belonged to someone who loved him. I wanted him to know that even though I am a predator, he was safe with me. Horses need to feel safe.

I let Scooter alone for a few weeks to get accustomed to his new home. I just fed him and checked the trough daily. He was now on acres of beautiful pasture with safe board fencing. He seemed content with his new equine buddies. The only time I saw fear rise up was when he saw me or another human. I didn't blame him.

I took Scooter's food and a book into the pasture. I left the bucket on the ground and walked twenty-five feet away. Too close for Scooter. He wasn't falling for that trick again. He stayed back by about seventy-five feet. He clearly wanted the grain, but not as much as freedom.

So I walked another seventy-five feet away and sat down in the grass. He approached the bucket and ate, popping his head up after every mouthful so I wouldn't sneak up on him. The next day I moved one hundred feet away, and I did that for three days, and then shortened the distance to seventy-five feet. I continued that pattern for three days, then moved closer, until he could handle me sitting and reading twelve feet away.

After several days of twelve feet, Scooter grew braver and crept forward to snuffle my book. I smiled but did not move.

Finally, after months, I could bring his bucket, wait for him to approach, drop the bucket, and touch his neck briefly. I would stroke him once and walk away. My goal was to *prove* that I was more interested in the relationship than anything else. He needed to know I would not catch him or force him. I wanted him to come to me because he wanted to. My job was to cause him to want to.

Almost five months later, I was able to invite him to come and accept the halter. At six months I decided to start Scooter in the round pen, where I could work with him in a more confined area.

It was a clear and cool October day with a northern blustery breeze. Scooter galloped around and around like a crazy thing, calling to his friends in the nearby pasture. I did not try to stop him from running, but I did begin stepping into his flight path to change his direction. A dozen or so direction changes caused him to look at me differently. His eyes grew softer, less fearful, more focused on me.

A gust of wind spooked him and he spurted forward, lost his footing, and fell on his right side, all four delicate legs poking through the steel entry gate of the round pen. Scooter lurched, trying to right himself, but could not get his legs out of the gate. He flailed, and I could foresee broken limbs.

I approached slowly and placed my hand on his neck. He stopped flailing. My knees hit the dirt, and I pressed my hand into his neck, asking him to lie flat. He did. I called my friend to walk slowly to the gate and open it. She did, but she was afraid to open the gate wide because Scooter would be able to run off when he rose. I told her to open it as wide as it would go. We had to free his legs.

Scooter just lay there—legs straight out in front. I feared he had already broken something. I stood up. Scooter did not move. I could feel my eyes burn as tears started. I knelt back down and got my fingers under his neck. "Come on, Scoots. Can you move?"

He raised his head.

I stood again and took a piece of his long mane in my fingers, inviting him to stand. He did. We just stood there for minutes, the gate wide open. I laid my arm over his neck like an old friend and invited him to walk with me a while. And he did.

That was twelve years ago.

And we are walking together still.

Ransom Delivered

Sarah Dowlearn

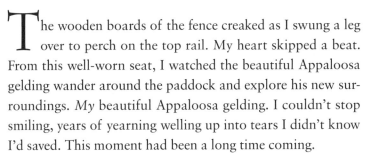

The wooden boards of the fence creaked as I swung a leg over to perch on the top rail. My heart skipped a beat. From this well-worn seat, I watched the beautiful Appaloosa gelding wander around the paddock and explore his new surroundings. *My* beautiful Appaloosa gelding. I couldn't stop smiling, years of yearning welling up into tears I didn't know I'd saved. This moment had been a long time coming.

I was six years old the first time I sprinted around the asphalt playground on Spangler, my imaginary horse. He was leopard patterned—white with small chestnut spots all over his body. We galloped around the drinking fountain, behind the kickball cage, and down the homestretch until a playground teacher grabbed my shoulder. "Don't run so fast."

Spangler screeched to a halt. I started to protest, but the bell rang. I left Spangler stabled next to the swings and filed back toward the classroom. Only an hour until lunch recess.

When I wasn't riding Spangler, I doodled horses all over my homework or pasted horse pictures into my scrapbooks. My idea of an art project was to make a feeder for my model horses and use corn silk for hay. I spent hours playing with my beloved Breyer and Grand Champion model horses, and I did extra chores around the house to save up to buy the newest one.

When I was eight, Grandma started sending me to horse camp. I lived for that one week every summer. After a couple of years, my camp instructor offered to let me stay around an extra week to help with the younger kids. She paid me twenty dollars—I'd never made so much money in my life—and I learned the invaluable skill of how to scoop poop. I started my horse savings fund with that paycheck. Nearly every dollar I made in the next six years went into the pickle jar with "horse owner" scrawled all over the lid. When I researched and presented a plan to my parents to fence our quarter acre, they took the hint and enrolled me in riding lessons instead.

Finances were tight, so every Saturday morning Momma dropped me off at 7:30 a.m. to work off partial payment for my lessons. I did everything—cleaning stalls, scrubbing water troughs, mucking paddocks, feeding, and helping with trail rides. My riding instructor badgered me. "Sarah, when are you going to get a horse?"

I thought of the meager contents of my jar and could only reply, "Not yet."

Despite my hard work and dreams of horse ownership, hope was at odds with reality. I knew my parents couldn't afford to buy a horse for me, and I didn't have so much as a bank account. The dream may have been tucked away under layers of rationality, but I'd never wanted anything so much. And I wanted it now.

As I waited, my teenage crush was an athletic Appaloosa lesson horse named Sonny. He let me tie ribbons in his mane for the Pink Ladies drill team and taught me to be a good rider. Good enough that when I went to college I competed on my school's equestrian team. During my college years the horse savings fund remained intact, though it had moved from a pickle jar to a savings account. But now every dollar earned went toward paying for school. My dream seemed buried even more.

In the summertime I worked as a wrangler at camp. My camp nickname was Spangles, based on my aging imaginary steed. Spangler still helped me demonstrate maneuvers to my students in the arena. Camp turned into a full-time job after graduation. The responsibilities and expenses of adulthood, as well as the nature of my job—pouring my time and energy into other people's horses—were quick to overwhelm any smidgen of hope that dared surface.

Then I made the mistake of browsing some on-line horse classified ads. The danger in that is you eventually find what you "aren't" looking for. This one jumped out at me through the computer screen the moment I saw the photo of his big spotted hip and kind eye. A quick scan confirmed he was also the right age and price, and in the right location. I pulled out my phone and dialed my mom.

"I just found my dream horse!"

The practical grown-up in me raised the familiar litany of reasons why it wouldn't work. But I looked at the ad the next day. And the next. And the day after that. I was scared to let myself hope, yet I had given the idea enough rein that it had taken the bit and run away with me.

If I had thought the timing was bad before, it couldn't have been worse now. In just a few months I would be moving to a new city, jobless, to be with family. Could I afford a horse until I found employment? Would the responsibility of horse ownership just add to the stress of the transition? What if I committed and then couldn't make it work?

My mind swirled with excitement and anxiety, until a single thought silenced the questions. *There is never going to be a perfect time. There is always going to be some good reason why circumstances aren't ideal.* That's when I knew my time was now.

That moment as I sat on the fence and watched, my first horse—the horse I'd waited for since I was six years old—fulfilled everything I'd imagined, everything I'd wanted. Was this really happening? I'd heard "not yet" for so long that I had to reset my dream to this new reality of "now."

No longer imaginary, my horse had a name: Ransom. He ambled over and nudged my knee with his nose. I rubbed the white star on his spotted face, looking at him with fresh eyes and a full soul. "Hey, handsome. Nice to meet you."

I brought Ransom home the same week I started packing to move. I said good-bye to many of my childhood horse treasures and thinned my model horse herd, trading them in for the real thing. Ransom had just as much character as any I gave them. Despite his prominent spine, he could flail like a roly-poly bug on its back. He loved napping on his bed of shavings and flirting with the beautiful black mare next door. He thought water troughs were meant for swimming. He still had the personable curiosity, honesty, and gangliness of a three-year-old. He helped me unlearn the emotional detachment I developed for working with horses on the job. Others commented on his scraggly black mane and tail, but I just shrugged. That was the genetic trade-off for spots—a sacrifice I didn't mind.

Ransom and I embarked on our new adventure together. The move was disjointed, and life had no rhythm, routine, or structure for several months. I'd wrapped my identity up in my work, and without it, I felt unmotivated and unproductive. Hunting for a job was tedious and often discouraging. All the while, I grieved for what I had left behind.

Ransom was the one bright spot during that difficult time. Driving out of the city into the canyon park where I boarded him was the only routine I had, one of the few reasons I had to get out of the house. He brought purpose to my otherwise aimless circumstances—I called it my Ransom therapy. I worked for the barn owner to barter my board, just like in the old days. Whenever I visited the barn, Ransom spied me from far off as I walked up the road toward his paddock. I knew the moment he saw me because his head came up and his eyes got bigger. One ear pricked toward me, while the other listened to the wind rustle the grass in waterless waves. When he nickered, I smiled. Really smiled. The discouragement of the day melted away in his warm breath and soft coat. The sacrifices I'd made to make this work were worth it.

When I finally landed a job at a therapeutic riding center, Ransom came with me. Only then did I look back on the previous months and realize that what I had thought was the worst timing turned out to be God's perfect timing. He knew Ransom was exactly the encouragement I would need during a difficult time of transition. He redeemed all those years of waiting and wanting, and his timing was perfect.

Snowbird

Rachel Anne Ridge

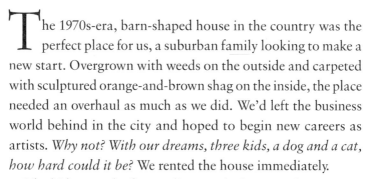

The 1970s-era, barn-shaped house in the country was the perfect place for us, a suburban family looking to make a new start. Overgrown with weeds on the outside and carpeted with sculptured orange-and-brown shag on the inside, the place needed an overhaul as much as we did. We'd left the business world behind in the city and hoped to begin new careers as artists. *Why not? With our dreams, three kids, a dog and a cat, how hard could it be?* We rented the house immediately.

The kids were the first to discover the barn on the property. Because it was obscured by brush and thistles as tall as a man, we hadn't even realized it was there when we signed the lease. The three burst through the door, all talking at once, eyes shining and excitement brimming.

"We have a barn out there! A real barn! Can we get a horse? Can we? Can we? We'll take care of it. We promise!" Their words tumbled out as they clamored for an immediate answer. "Please, please, please, please?"

Suddenly my girlhood dreams of owning a horse came rushing back to me like a tidal wave. I remembered combing the newspapers for horses in the livestock section of the want ads and begging my parents daily for a horse. *Please, please, please, please?* I could just picture my mare: she'd be black and white, like Little Joe's horse on *Bonanza*. Never mind that we lived in town, with a small backyard and no barn. No matter that we didn't know the first thing about horses. I only knew that my love for my future horse could surmount these small obstacles. But year after year, reality gradually replaced my dream, and I accepted the sadness of never being able to have a horse of my own. We were a city family. It was not meant to be.

But now, here we were in the country, with a perfectly good barn. Three stalls. Sturdy structure. Six acres of pasture.

Destiny called.

The kids and I launched a horse campaign. I started reading the ads and bringing up the subject whenever possible.

My husband, Tom, who owned a pony as a child, was open to the idea but hesitant. He knew the amount of time and commitment it would take, and he felt the novelty might wear off more quickly than we might think. He suggested we *borrow* a horse for a while and see how it went before we actually bought one. If we kept up with the responsibility and enjoyed horsemanship as much as we hoped, then we would look for just the right horse to purchase.

Deal. We were elated.

Some friends of ours had a horse they were no longer riding— Snowbird, a white mare. She was older, they said, almost thirty, and a little bit slow. But she'd once been a competition horse—a champion barrel racer—and she was smart and good with new riders. They would be glad to let us keep her for a while and even offered the use of tack so we could ride immediately. She sounded perfect. So we cleaned up the barn and made arrangements for Snowbird to arrive.

The truck and trailer pulled up late in the afternoon that March day. We could see a white muzzle poking through the small window as our friend walked around to unlatch the trailer door. Our excitement mounted. The door swung open, and out backed Snowbird on her own. She was a pro.

With all four feet on the ground, she swung around, and we got our first look at her.

Oh dear.

Our friends had neglected to mention that Snowbird was one step from the grave. Her back swayed low, leaving her withers and hips unnaturally high. Her lower lip sagged, which gave her a perennially sad expression. Her coat seemed patchy and dull, and her head sort of hung down in resignation to the age that had caught up with her. Not exactly Little Joe's spiffy steed.

> *"Horses make a landscape look beautiful."*
> ALICE WALKER

We stepped forward to meet Snowbird, and she eyed us warily, sizing up the situation and realizing instantly that we were greenhorns. With a snort, she turned to inspect her new surroundings, and I knew we'd made a huge mistake. This girl was too far past her prime to teach us anything. I tried to hide my disappointment.

"Give her a flake and a half of hay each evening when you put her up in the stall for the night. A cup of sweet feed, water, and you're good to go." The man scrawled a few more instructions on a small scrap of paper, stuck it to the saddle, and then they were off, leaving us with Snowbird and the name of a local farrier.

We were eager to try riding her. And that's when we began to discover just how clever she was. The first challenge was to catch her. For an old lady, she sure was elusive. She had loved having long afternoons with nothing to do, no one to bother her, no job to accomplish, nowhere to go. The retirement life suited her just fine. So she did not appreciate being disrupted from her daily "Won't Do" list to get a bridle on. In fact, the fastest we ever saw her move was to get away from Tom, who had to bring his roping skills up to speed to bring her in.

Once the bridle was on, the next trick was to saddle up. No matter how tight we cinched her, the moment our feet were in the stirrups, the saddle started to slide. She had perfected the art of bloating and holding her breath while being saddled, and she loved it when we'd start to slide off to the side mid-trot.

And somehow, Snowbird knew how to cut our rides short. She pretended to stumble. A surefooted animal at all other times, she stumbled only when she had a rider. This, of course, scared us newbie riders into hopping off sooner than we would have liked. I could almost hear Snowbird stifle a snicker. I sighed in defeat as I pulled the saddle from her back and released her to the pasture.

Taking care of an old horse we could barely ride was not much fun. We began to argue about whose turn it was to feed and brush her. Cleaning out her stall was a chore nobody wanted. I didn't spend nearly as much time with Snowbird as I thought I would. She was a bit of a burden, and I looked forward to returning her to her owners.

One morning it was our daughter Meghan's turn to let Snowbird out of the barn and muck the stall. She had been gone only a couple of minutes when she returned, a look of horror on her face.

"Snowbird's gone!" she said. "I can't find her anywhere!"

Snowbird's owners also neglected to tell us that, apparently, she could open latches with her teeth. Which would not have been a problem had we left the *outside* gate closed. Then she would have remained safely in the pasture. Unfortunately, someone had been careless and trusted the one-barricade system to work. With the stall door unlatched and the gate wide open, Snowbird waltzed her way to freedom. *But where did she go?*

A frantic search ensued. We fanned out over our property and up and down the road. We called and shook coffee cans with oats inside. We looked high and low with no sign of her. By this time the sun was hot overhead, and I imagined her lying dead somewhere. *Oh dear Lord, please, no.* What would I say to her owners? How could I explain this one? I couldn't help it: I looked into the sky to see if there were vultures circling nearby. *Fingers crossed.* None so far. Good.

We regrouped over lunch to strategize our afternoon search. Just then the phone rang. It was our daughter's friend, who lived several miles down the road. She happened to mention that some random horse walked by and that her father had put her into their pasture for safekeeping.

Snowbird!

We left our half-eaten lunch and bolted out the door. Driving down the winding road, across the bridge, through the woods, and past several country neighborhoods and ranches, we marveled at how far Snowbird had wandered. We finally arrived at our destination, where the man who rescued her was leaning against a fence, waiting for us.

"Well, I'm sure glad you're here!" he said with a chuckle. "That old gal's got some spice in her, I'll tell you what." We glanced over at Snowbird, who looked almost unrecognizable. Why, she must have shed fifteen years on her walk! Head held high and tail swishing, she trotted back and forth along the fence . . . to the delight of the three young stallions in the next pen. She tossed her head and gave a whinny, sidestepping to show her best side. The three young bucks clamored for a look, eager to see Snowbird's show. She looked almost lovely.

"Yep, your mare must have sensed I had these boys here, because she made a beeline for 'em and has been teasing them all morning." He adjusted his cowboy hat over his eyes and led us to the gate. Tom unwound the lead rope and, with a shake of the oat can, brought Snowbird up close to put her halter on. She wasn't happy about leaving her admiring audience, but she dutifully loaded up into the trailer to head home, like a pro.

As we opened the door for Snowbird to back herself out, we had a new perspective on our old, borrowed horse. Up close, the afternoon sun showed her age and wear. Her lower lip hung down once again, and she sighed as her adventure came to a close. But somehow, we saw a spark in her eyes we hadn't noticed before. We had a glimpse of the showgirl she'd once been, and suddenly, we admired her grace and spirit. Had she had that sparkle the whole time and I'd never noticed? I reached up and took her face in my hands and rubbed her nose. Her ears pricked forward and she held my gaze for a long while.

"You silly thing!" I said. "You are full of surprises, aren't you?"

Snowbird seemed to nod her head in agreement. I ran my hand down her neck and gave her a pat, releasing her to find her water bucket. I watched her amble away, hips jutting but steps sure.

There was more to Snowbird than I had thought. It took a group of three young stallions and an old cowboy to help me realize it. I'd been wrong to judge her "too old" to be good for anything. I'd only seen her shabby outside and not taken the time to see her beauty inside. I'd been so disappointed in being loaned a retired horse that I failed to appreciate her soul. I had focused on the chores involved in her care rather than on the joy of connecting with an animal who had given years of her life for the enjoyment of others. She deserved better, and I let her down. I was glad we had several more months together to make up for lost time.

Snowbird still had her willful ways of avoiding long rides. We still had to work to catch her. We had to mind the gate latches. But she loved being groomed and enjoyed the attention we gave her. She was gentle and patient with people who had little experience around horses. Her warm brown eyes conveyed her gratitude and affection.

Snowbird taught us about horsemanship and a little something about life. She taught a city family about the joys of country living: How to muck out a stall. How to pick out a hoof. How to cinch a saddle. How to appreciate the simple pleasures of the smell of hay and a fresh bag of oats. We learned what it means to take care of an equine—a grand animal who trusts in her caregivers and gives love and joy in return. We learned that caring for something important takes time and commitment

34

and can have intrinsic, lasting rewards. Snowbird taught us that older doesn't mean "not useful," but valuable and precious. It's the spark inside, that soul that is eternally young, that connects us to one another.

I'm forever grateful to an old, borrowed horse named Snowbird for teaching us that it's not the cover that counts, but the pages within. There is beauty to be found in every living being, no matter the age or outward appearance.

You must simply look for it, and you'll find it waiting to be discovered.

The Day the Horse Confirmed What Is Real

Lonnie Hull DuPont

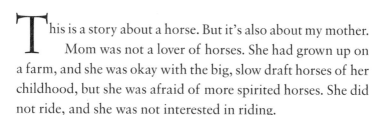

This is a story about a horse. But it's also about my mother. Mom was not a lover of horses. She had grown up on a farm, and she was okay with the big, slow draft horses of her childhood, but she was afraid of more spirited horses. She did not ride, and she was not interested in riding.

My sister, on the other hand, was what we called "horse-crazy," and fortunately for her, Mom accepted that horse craziness and allowed us to have horses. Although Mom thought horses were scary, she also thought they were pretty to look at. So she enjoyed their beauty from a respectable distance—from her kitchen window.

While I was growing up, we had one or a few horses at any given time. I rode them and worked in the barns. But for me, horses were more pets than passion. I loved our horses and have many happy memories attached to being around them. My older sister, however, had that adolescent girl's love for her palomino.

The palomino was named, appropriately enough, Pal. He was a large, gorgeous gelding. He was a nice creature and easy to ride—until he'd get it in his head that he was done having someone on his back. When he was done, he was done. Then he was no longer easy to ride. He would take off for home—fast.

I had the scary experience myself of Pal being done with someone on his back. I was riding him down the road and had gone about a quarter mile when he suddenly spun around and headed for home at a gallop. I was only eleven at the time and not the good rider my sister was, but I managed to stay seated. I saw he was headed for the hay manger, and as we approached the small barn that housed it, I ducked so as not to be knocked off by a beam. Once inside, Pal stopped dead in his tracks, which almost threw me off him. Then he began munching on hay as if nothing unusual had happened. I dismounted with shaky legs. I never enjoyed riding him after that. I didn't trust him, and I didn't have the experience to handle such behavior.

One day I was playing in the yard and noticed my sister riding Pal. But something was amiss. They were nowhere near the barn or the road; rather, they were headed through the backyard toward the house, a route we never took on horseback. I quickly realized there was trouble, because Pal was in a dead run. He had on only a halter and a dangling lead rope, and he had clearly done one of his taking-off numbers. My sister—only fourteen at the time—ducked low on his back and clung to his mane. That was all she could do.

Let me hit the pause button for just a moment and tell you that my sister and I were each adopted in our infancies. This was in the fifties, when people didn't talk much about such things.

But fortunately our parents told us, even before we were able to understand the word *adopted*, that that's what we were—and were they ever glad about it, they let us know. "The luckiest day of our lives," they would say, "was the day we got you."

And while our parents had their problems and eventually divorced, they stayed of one mind regarding how to handle our adoptions—always positively and lovingly. I never wondered if I was their "real" daughter. I knew I had another biological family out there, but I also knew I was absolutely and legitimately the daughter of my folks who adopted me. My sister felt the same.

I happened to be very close to Mom. We had that spiritual bond a parent and child can have. Once I said to her, "I have no way of proving this, but I don't believe a mother and daughter related by blood could be any closer than you and I are." She agreed wholeheartedly.

But how does one confirm such a thing?

Let's go back to my sister and her horse, running through the yard . . .

Pal headed for a dip in the lawn that ran between the old stone smokehouse and a huge catalpa tree standing next to the house just outside the kitchen. Things looked bad for my sister—and possibly bad for Pal, given the fact that the dangling rope was bouncing alongside his running legs.

Suddenly the kitchen door swung open, and my mother charged out of the house. This woman, so timid around livestock, took five long steps to the spot in the path where Pal was headed. As the horse was about to race by her, Mom reached out, grabbed the dangling lead rope, and yanked that big beast around, stopping him in his tracks.

It was jaw-dropping.

And it was something else. If ever I wondered if we children were "real"—if my mother loved us the way a "real" mother loves—I clearly did not need to. When provoked, Mom was a fierce mother bear whose fear would not stop her from protecting us.

My mother stepped right into the path of a running, out-of-control horse to save her child.

Desires of a Heart

Cynthia Beach

The book cover convinced me. I needed a horse. A black one. My sister Laur's Scholastic book, Walter Farley's *The Black Stallion and the Girl*, depicted a girl whose blonde hair blew toward the black horse who stood near her. The only drawback? I was a first grader living in San Jose, California. How could I ever have a horse?

But nothing deterred my love of horses. By fourth grade I had read all the library's horse stories. At recess I even became a horse. In black patent leather shoes—required by my private school—I clacked across blacktop. At home Breyer model horses crowded two shelves over my twin bed. Stretched across my door was a full-size horse mural. And somewhere a black horse in its stall waited for me to grow.

After I turned thirteen, my family had moved to the more rural Los Gatos. One day Mom and Dad arrived home late from their work at the dental office. Laur and I caught them in the kitchen looking oddly mischievous. Instead of their usual work clothes, they wore an unusual getup: jeans and boots.

"Where were you?" I charged.

Mom and Dad exchanged little grins. "Well," Mom said, "we were looking for horses for you girls."

Joy erupted. I caught my sister's hands and we jigged. We were getting horses.

The moment finally came when I would meet Chicobi, a seven-year-old horse. Mom explained that this Arabian quarter horse was a small gelding in need of a good home. Although it took less than an hour, the drive to the ranch where he was seemed like a cross-country trip. When we arrived, I spotted the red horse beyond the boards of a dusty corral, an English saddle on his back.

When I settled into that saddle, every nerve in my body hummed. Chicobi heeded my leg pressure. He was responsive, well-behaved. The owner asked me if I wanted to canter. I pressed my legs tighter, and Chicobi glided into a rippling canter. I knew this was the horse I wanted.

Soon Laur and I were bicycling down Shannon Road every day possible to spend hours brushing and riding our horses, Chicobi and Kawiki. My horse love focused like a laser on Chicobi. While his coat wasn't dreamy black, it didn't matter much. His red coat sparkled in the sun. Besides, he was mine.

But my dreams had led me to believe I was an expert horsewoman, which I wasn't. The longer I owned Chicobi, the more I noticed his strength and will. I began having more and more incidents with him when he'd take the bit and run.

Then one February day, Chicobi overpowered me and ran downhill through a plum orchard. My head cracked against a limb; I awoke on my back, confused. Had I come up the hill to take a nap? But what was the warm, wet feel on my face?

The seventy-two stitches that united my cheek left the plastic surgeon marveling I had any feeling there at all. A severe concussion sent me to the hospital for three days, my head wrapped like a mummy's.

While my young body repaired itself, my psyche did not. Anything faster than a walk astride Chicobi or another horse pushed sweat into my palms. Fear corroded my horse passion.

Decades then passed. Another move took me cross-country to Michigan with my husband. Chicobi had long since passed from my life. The girl who loved black horses was now middle-aged.

A new friend came into my life. Wanda owned Stone Creek Ranch, only minutes away. The first time I drove her pasture-lined driveway, something within me lifted. Horses filled her green pastures. Soon Wanda introduced me to a black Friesian, Assante, whose dark mane waved from his crested neck. I was smitten. He was also the most expensive horse on the lot. Purebred Friesians were worth well over $10,000. I would never own a Friesian. Impossible.

Wanda grinned. "You're welcome anytime to come over and groom him."

She repeated this invite until I believed her, which took some time. Fear collided with desire. I felt timid around horses. But the day I led Assante from his pasture, the girl within me awoke.

Wanda wasn't content, however. My lasting fear intrigued her. She wanted to work with me to heal it. So astride Assante, I began to regain my confidence and love.

Soon Wanda gave me Melissa Sovey-Nelson's *If I Had a Horse How Different Life Would Be*. The title alone may have set me to dreaming, but the book also offered picture after picture of prancing black Friesians. On its pages, I read Phyllis

Theroux's words: "One of the earliest religious disappointments in a young girl's life devolves upon her unanswered prayer for a horse."[2] That hadn't been my story. I had gotten my horse. But something within my grand passion had broken. I had translated a horrific accident into a mantra: *Don't trust dreams. They hurt. They'll disappoint you every time.*

My adult life further underscored this dour belief. My husband's midlife career change hadn't brought the success or income we had expected. My novel manuscript—a ten-year endeavor—had reaped only "no thank you." Several times.

I continued thumbing through the book Wanda gave me. Sandwiched between three pictures of black Friesians, I read, "There is always a reason a horse appears in a woman's life . . . they often catch us off guard with the possibility of new horizons and secret gates to our souls that need unlocking."[3]

It could never be, I thought. Sure, we had a pasture and a small barn where we boarded a neighbor's horse. But a horse of my own? We didn't have the money. Maybe in ten years.

And then it came—a forwarded email from Wanda. She prefaced it, "Cynthia, I thought of you when I read this! I think this horse is for you. I know you said you aren't ready . . . but pray about the desire of your heart."

The desire of my heart?

My gaze traveled to the forwarded email's subject line. I read, "Beautiful horse to be donated." A picture showed the horse. The leggy gelding wore a coat of crow-black. *Don't bother*, I thought. It would never happen.

The owner, a woman from Ohio named Jane, described the horse, Gentleman Jet. He was part Tennessee Walker—and part Friesian. His owner had bought him for her husband although Gent showed a slight limp. The seller assured her that the lameness came after two days of hard riding. "For some reason," Jane explained, "I just 'knew' in my heart that I should buy him."

After a month of continued lameness and a visit to the vet, Jane learned Gent had ringbone, an arthritis common in older horses. She wrote, "At that point I really had to question that knowing I had in my heart. 'God, why did I believe that I should buy this horse? That makes me really doubt hearing that small voice.' What I heard back was, 'Maybe you didn't buy him for you.'"

Jane explained that she wanted Gent used in a program for helping people. While she said he ought not to be ridden, he could serve well in a ground program—"or where folks just need a horse to love on." She concluded, "My greatest desire is that he could make a difference in someone's life."

Both Wanda and my husband, Dave, whose counseling practice included equine therapy, emailed Jane and told her why I should be the one to own this horse because of my broken horse love and because Dave could use Gent in therapy sessions. My hope lifted—what if?

But the beautiful gelding had attracted more demand around the Midwest than Jane had anticipated. She sent a mass email: "I'm going to pray about it."

I waited and waited. Finally a week passed; I knew I wasn't going to be chosen. The next morning I awoke and, over coffee, checked email. A new email bore Jane's address. I readied myself.

She had picked a person and that person was . . . me. When would I like Gentleman Jet to arrive?

I closed the email, saved it, and paced the kitchen before reopening it. Jane's words hadn't changed. Gent was mine. Joy like the day Mom and Dad surprised us surged through me.

Rain pelted us the day Gent would arrive at my Michigan home. Wanda and her husband joined us for the wait. Laur came too, carrying the box of Breyer model horses that had once lined the shelves above my twin bed. As Jane's estimated arrival time approached, I carried a dining room chair to the front window and sat facing the road. I could not talk. Excitement supercharged me.

And then a white pickup with a matching horse trailer pulled up our dirt road. My family and friends gathered around me before we darted into the downpour to meet Gentleman Jet. As I waited outside with rain sloshing off my slicker, I had one last negative thought that he probably wasn't as good-looking as his picture.

Jane stopped and shook hands with me. She was a short woman with an open face. Then she disappeared into the shadowy trailer. I couldn't see Gent yet. Moments later Jane reemerged. A long-legged black horse, tall and athletic, stepped onto my driveway and looked around. He had the height and stance of a Walker with a Friesian's haunches, tail, and ebony color. Gentleman Jet was model-horse perfect. The desire of my heart had arrived. Joy scoured away the residue of disappointments with dreams.

Three decades after the riding accident, that still-horse-crazy-middle-aged girl got a black horse. He stands in my pasture and reminds me: Someone loves the desires of my heart.

Amish Buggy Horses

If you spot a yellow traffic sign with a black horse and buggy on it, you know you're in Amish country. Together, the horse and buggy are an Amish icon.

Let's take this a step further. Suppose you see a horse and buggy driving on the road. If you're knowledgeable about horses, you're probably aware that the buggy horse is a Standardbred or Thoroughbred. You might observe that the horse seems to enjoy its job. But most don't realize that a buggy horse began its life in a racing stable.

Racetrack horses usually have a very short racing life. After they're retired from the racetrack, these four- to six-year-old horses are sold at auctions; many end up on Amish farms. They're ideally suited for the job—young, strong, capable, and conditioned to loud, unexpected noises.

The one concern that requires additional training, Amish horsemen say, is that racehorses are encouraged to bolt—to run for the finish line. Traffic conditioning reins in that natural impulse. Once trained, a buggy horse becomes like a beloved family member, well cared for and highly valued, toting the family around for years. As one Amish bishop said, "The only way we can repay the animals in our care is with kindness."

Suzanne Woods Fisher

My MacIntosh

Audrey Leach

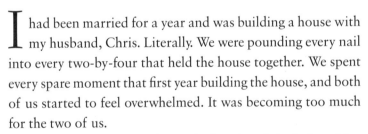

I had been married for a year and was building a house with my husband, Chris. Literally. We were pounding every nail into every two-by-four that held the house together. We spent every spare moment that first year building the house, and both of us started to feel overwhelmed. It was becoming too much for the two of us.

One Saturday I was tired—tired of work and tired of working on the house. While driving that day, I saw a painted wooden sign I'd not noticed before:

"Horse for Sale—$150."

Wow, I thought, *I want that horse.*

I dismissed the idea as a want, not a need—and we needed so many other things right then. On top of everything going on at the house, my father-in-law, Richard, was having serious problems with his heart.

In the next few days, I drove by the sign several times. One day I stopped in. The owners took me to their barn and introduced me to a beautiful buckskin mare they called Tasha. She stood in the corner of the barn with her head down and looking none too happy. I draped my arms over the fence and *chic-chic*-ed her over (horse talk for "Hey—hello! Come here!").

Tasha looked up and walked over to me. She had four black stockings, one with a little bit of white, the most beautiful black mane and tail, and a little white blaze on her forehead. I stood next to her, and my head hit her front shoulder. *Just the right size.* She placed her nose next to my ear, breathed out, and nickered.

I knew in an instant I was buying this horse. I did not care what it took, I was doing it. Horses are herd animals, and Tasha and I had found our herd—together. She was my kindred spirit. I did not care that we needed carpet, kitchen cabinets, and a washer. This horse needed me and I needed her. I believed she had been given the wrong name, and Tasha became MacIntosh. I made arrangements to pick her up later.

Of course, when I told Chris, he thought I was crazy. He stared at me and said, "With all we have going on, you want a horse?"

I guess I did not think it through very well. I only knew MacIntosh had to come home with me. We did not have a barn, we did not have a fence, and we did not have a water trough. We did have fifteen acres, though. What else did a horse really need? Chris finally accepted the idea.

Saturday arrived. I borrowed a saddle and rode my new horse the three miles home. It was a gorgeous

48

spring day, perfect for riding. No work, no house building, no worries about my father-in-law's health or my husband's state of mind over it. It was enough to have the sun on my back as MacIntosh clip-clopped down the road. I had the sense of being in the moment. I felt at peace.

It took a half day of work for Chris and me to get the fence posts in and wire strung for an electric fence. MacIntosh looked beautiful on our rolling hill. From that day on, I would get up every Saturday in the early morning and ride a few miles down our gravel road, then brush MacIntosh and feed her. I would forget about work, forget about building the house. Forget my wants, forget my needs. Forget to worry about my father-in-law. I would simply drift in thought, living in the here and now.

One night as I was drifting off to sleep, I heard something knock up against the bedroom wall. I thought someone was breaking in. I shook Chris and whispered, "Get up! Someone's outside!"

Chris jumped up and looked out the window, then went to the front door with me behind him holding his T-shirt—it made me feel safe. We turned on the outside light, and there was MacIntosh reclining—yes, lying down—under our bedroom window. I do not know to this day how she managed to get out of the fenced-in area. But I guess some things you don't question. MacIntosh wanted to be close to us. We were her herd, and she wanted to be a part of it.

Another time MacIntosh came up to the living room windows as we were watching television. She stood and watched with us—the entire program. When it was time for us to go to bed, she moseyed over to the bedroom window, and down she lay.

In the meantime my father-in-law's heart problems progressed quickly. Open heart surgery was required, and he survived a triple bypass. When Chris and I went to see Richard in the hospital, the doctor said he needed to walk as much as he could and as soon as possible. When Richard went home a few days later, Chris and I went to visit him at his house. He sat on the patio in the sun and was feeling pretty down.

Chris and I urged Richard to come with us to walk around our land. At first he was having none of it, but we finally convinced him it would help him recover faster if he got moving again. We drove Richard to our place. He had not yet met MacIntosh, and we entered the pasture.

> "The outside of a horse is good for the inside of a man."
> WINSTON CHURCHILL

MacIntosh came to us, nuzzled Richard's chest, and nickered. Since Richard was still unsteady on his feet, he turned his back to her. MacIntosh lowered her head and nudged him to take a step. He shot her a warning look, but he took a step. She lowered her head and nudged him again until he took two more steps. She then walked alongside him. Richard rested his forearm on MacIntosh's back, and they proceeded to walk side by side around the pasture.

It was a breakthrough for Richard. He continued to go walking with MacIntosh around the pasture, and it became a huge part of his rehabilitation. We watched the horse help Richard get back his confidence to get on with life. One day as Chris and I watched his father walk with MacIntosh around the pasture, Chris said to me, "You know, you could have paid off the washer or bought carpet with that money. I am glad you did something for yourself by buying MacIntosh."

It confirmed for me that it's okay sometimes to do something that doesn't seem to make sense at the time. MacIntosh helped my father-in-law recover. MacIntosh taught me how to let go of my worry. MacIntosh gave me a peace of mind.

So if you ever see a painted wooden sign with the words "Horse for Sale," you just might find a kindred spirit to fit into your herd. And with it, you may receive much more than you thought you would ever need . . . or want, for that matter.

A Horse Named Gentle Breeze

Sherri Gallagher

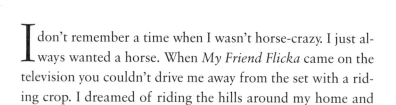

I don't remember a time when I wasn't horse-crazy. I just always wanted a horse. When *My Friend Flicka* came on the television you couldn't drive me away from the set with a riding crop. I dreamed of riding the hills around my home and having adventures.

In eighth grade I changed schools. I wore thick glasses and no makeup. I loved the outdoors and animals, had excellent grades, and refused to let people cheat off my tests. All in all, I was the kind of girl no one wanted for a friend.

One lunch I sat trying to sketch a horse and making a real mess of it. The head was okay, but the back leg was twice the size of the rest of my drawing. Another girl in my class, Cheryl, glanced over my shoulder.

"Move the hock up higher and it will fit better."

I glanced up, more than a little surprised that someone would consent to talk to me. "Thanks."

Cheryl sat down on the bench next to me. "Do you have a horse?"

"No. I wish I did. Do you?"

"Yeah, we have thirty head of horses grazing on about three hundred acres. Would you like to come ride sometime?"

"I'd love it." Visions of groomed and well-mannered horses galloped through my thoughts.

Cheryl nodded and walked away. I wondered if she meant the offer or if she was playing games with me. At least her recommendation made my drawing a little better.

But Cheryl invited me over to ride that weekend. I was so excited my stomach flipped and flopped until I thought I would lose my breakfast. I skipped and danced into the barn at Cheryl's, where a double row of horses stood in stalls with funny containers strapped to their bodies.

"What are the horses wearing?"

Cheryl took a deep breath, and she looked like she was preparing for an argument. "They collect urine from the pregnant mares. My dad sells it to the pharmaceutical companies, and they extract the hormones for medicine. That's why we have so many horses."

I nodded and let my scientific curiosity run wild. "I wonder how they do the extraction. Do you think a centrifuge would do it?"

Cheryl relaxed and smiled. Later I would find out that she wanted to study medicine. "I don't know. I wanted a tour, but they said no."

"Are the horses we're riding pregnant? Do we need to do anything different to be nice to them?"

"We're riding Glory and Zephyr, and no, they haven't been bred."

53

Cheryl carefully tacked both horses and gave me a leg up onto Zephyr. She checked my stirrups and handed me the reins. Throughout all of it Zephyr stood quietly, head down and half asleep. She occasionally stomped to dislodge a fly.

After she was sure all was correct, Cheryl nonchalantly announced, "I forgot to tell you Zephyr is a retired barrel racer," and she proceeded to give the horse a slap on the rump.

Zephyr went from sleepy head down to head-up, flat-out, down-the-homestretch gallop. Novice rider that I was, I pulled back on the reins. She just seemed to go faster. We flew at a huge fence that got bigger with every stride of my mount. I finally decided there was no way she was going to be able to stop and she must be planning on jumping. I grabbed a handful of mane, squeezed my legs as tight as I could, and prepared to stick like a wad of gum to that saddle. At the very last instant, Zephyr dropped down on her haunches, locked her front legs, and slid to a stop. She looked like a dog sitting down. Then she calmly stood and started to crop grass. I shook too much to even think about climbing out of that saddle.

Cheryl trotted up on Glory, a big grin on her face. "Okay, now I know how much riding experience you have. If a horse ever runs away with you, saw on the reins, don't just pull back."

"What do you mean?" My voice was little more than a whisper.

Cheryl took a rein in each hand to demonstrate. "Pull first on the right rein, then on the left. Try to make the horse's head go at a different rhythm than the hoofbeats. They can't handle the difference, and even if they hold the bit with their teeth, they have to slow down and stop."

She slid from the saddle and motioned me to get down. "You ride Glory, and I'll take Zephyr. Glory takes good care of her rider."

That cemented our friendship.

Cheryl had to do lots of chores related to the horses and her parents' business. While she was prettier than me, her lack of participation at school kept her from having other friends. Just being around horses was a thrill for me, and I considered hauling buckets of water and shoveling stalls to be fun. With my help, Cheryl had more free time, and we were able to ride a couple of times a week. Working together also put our grades at the top of the class academically.

Winter closed in and icy conditions made riding too dangerous. Cheryl and I made the best of it with plans for "as soon as it thaws," so it was no wonder that on this particular warm April afternoon we were more than just a little distracted and prone to trouble.

The substitute teacher pointed to the chalkboard. "All right, class, our last spelling word is *zephyr*. It means a gentle breeze."

Cheryl and I exchanged glances and burst out laughing. My notebook toppled to the floor with a loud thump while tears ran down Cheryl's face. She slid down in her seat until only her eyes and the top of her head were visible above the desk.

The teacher turned to glare at us. "Care to share the joke, ladies?"

We exchanged looks again and tried to swallow giggles. I finally managed to choke out, "That's the name of one of Cheryl's horses."

Another exchange of looks and we both dissolved into more guffaws. The teacher's quizzical expression set off additional waves of laughter. The bell rang and we tried to escape in the mob exiting this last class of the day.

"Cheryl and Sherri, come here."

Oh boy, we were in for it. Careful not to look at each other, we shuffled up to the teacher's desk, hugging our notebooks like shields and trying to stifle the giggles that kept bubbling up in our throats.

"I am truly disappointed in you. I was left a note that in all the class I could depend on you two girls not to be rude or pull pranks. Now explain yourselves."

When Cheryl got nervous she clammed up. It was up to me to straighten things out, but how did I explain about Zephyr? She was more than just a horse; she was Cheryl's test to qualify as a friend and our ticket to freedom and sights we could never get to on foot. How did I put all that into words?

I chewed on a chipped fingernail. "We're sorry. You see, Cheryl has a horse named Zephyr and well, she kind of has two speeds—stock-still or flat-out, blow-your-hat-off gallop. We thought her name meant a hurricane or at least a gale, so when you said 'gentle breeze,' it just didn't fit with the horse we know."

The sub stared at us for an eternity. Sweat trickled down my back as I waited to see if we would get a detention. How would I explain to Mom and Dad? The teacher was always right. If I got a punishment in school, another one would be waiting when I got home.

She nodded. "Go ride your crazy horse."

Cheryl and I bolted for the door.

"Hey, Mr. F is going to be gone all week and we don't have any tests, so let's ride tomorrow," Cheryl offered as we hurried to our lockers.

Skipping school sounded like the safest alternative after today. Besides, we both had straight-A averages in all our classes, and it was spring. We had gone months without playing hooky, and hadn't the sub just told us to go ride? "I'm in."

Cheryl called and made sure our cohort in crime, her grandfather, was up to the challenge of springing us from home. We found out years later that he had discussed all this with our parents. As long as Gramps did the driving and our grades didn't suffer, our parents accepted our phony stomachaches and ignored the occasional smell of horses when we came home.

Under Gramps's supervision, we would ride all day with breaks for peanut butter and dill pickle sandwiches, Glory's favorite, and soda. Later in the afternoon Cheryl's grandmother would appear with a platter of cookies and glasses of cold milk. While we took a break from horses, Gramps would have us crack open our schoolbooks and make sure we understood the lessons. Gramps always had us home in time to get rid of the smell of horses, or try to, and to do whatever chores had been left for us by our parents.

Cheryl called later that night. "Gramps will give us a ride."

It had been my turn to review our homework for the next day. We didn't want any unpleasant surprises or *F* grades, or our mini vacations would be over. "Great. Tomorrow's math assignment is easy. Let's get it done tonight so all we have left is the English essay. That way we can get more riding in."

"Or brush more. Gramps said the horses have been rolling in the mud to get rid of their winter coats," Cheryl answered with a laugh.

I waited in the doorway for our trusty blue chariot and climbed into the backseat as soon as it rolled to a stop. Gramps tested our understanding of right and isosceles triangles in between our singing along to the Beatles songs playing on the radio.

We raced out of the car, leaving our books for Gramps to take inside. Grabbing a bucket of sweet feed, we headed into the pasture and quickly collected our mounts. An hour later our motley equines were ready. Long winter coats stuck out in patches next to shiny summer undercoats. About the best that could be said was the mud was off the horses and liberally distributed on us. I cleaned my glasses on the tail of my shirt; it had been tucked inside my jeans so it was slightly cleaner than the rest of me. I remembered my daydreams of a picturesque herd of horses, all clean and shiny. I laughed at the reality.

For this ride we took off into the fields across the road, ducking low on our horses' necks and sharing gossip and giggles as we cut through the forest. We broke out into a clearing and stopped to rest the horses and our aching leg muscles before riding up the next hill.

In front of us was a mass of wild violets. The bright purple flowers coated the ground, and the only other vegetation were wild apple trees in full bloom. The picture of the entire hillside rising up in front of us with white-limned, black-limbed trees and the deep-violet ground peeking through stunned us into silence. We rode up into the trees, finally stopping. All around us were the white blossoming branches. It felt like being in a cloud made up of flowers. The sweet smell from the violets we crushed with each step rose up to envelop us in its delicate scent.

"Hey, let's lie down and see what the sky looks like from the violets' point of view," Cheryl said.

I slid out of the saddle to land with a squish. Water seeped up through the flowers and covered the toes of my riding boots. Cheryl landed with a similar splash. I held the reins and looked over at my friend. "I don't know about you, but I'm scuzzy enough as it is without having a wet seat for the rest of the day."

Cheryl nodded and handed me a sandwich from her saddlebags. I passed her a soda from mine. We ate leaning against the trees and catching ourselves as we nearly fell over trying to look up at the blue sky through the masses of blossoms.

The horses were less impressed and settled in to graze, turning their bits into slimy green and purple messes. We tried to collect some violets to take back to Cheryl's grandmother, but their fragile stems and petals didn't survive the picking process. We would simply have to remember this beautiful gift. We climbed back aboard our trusty steeds to explore some more.

Several hours later we settled in with warm oatmeal cookies, milk, and our English project: write an essay describing springtime and use as many of the spelling words as possible. At least Cheryl and I had no trouble finding a use for the name *Zephyr*; describing the violets and apple blossoms was another thing.

We survived the rest of the term, with only rare calls to Gramps for a hooky break, and headed into summer with all the excitement of your normal, average teenager. Beyond housework and helping my milkman dad occasionally, my time was my own, and Gramps's old station wagon would chug into my driveway two or three times a week with Cheryl riding shotgun. We would escape into the fields that surrounded his house, sure that our trusty mounts would take us anywhere we asked.

That was one lovely summer. We spent our time swimming in the pond while the horses grazed nearby. We shared our sandwiches with Glory and Zephyr and dreamed of what we would be when we grew up. Glory and Zephyr weren't anything special, just grade horses, but they gave us our freedom and the confidence to step out and take the chances needed to be successful. And a friendship that has lasted a lifetime.

Mom and the Race Horse

Claudia Wolfe St. Clair

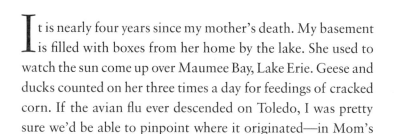

It is nearly four years since my mother's death. My basement is filled with boxes from her home by the lake. She used to watch the sun come up over Maumee Bay, Lake Erie. Geese and ducks counted on her three times a day for feedings of cracked corn. If the avian flu ever descended on Toledo, I was pretty sure we'd be able to pinpoint where it originated—in Mom's front yard.

I should tell you, my mother was a great lover of animals and wildlife. She spoke to every dog, cat, and squirrel on her neighborhood walks. Her pockets were always full of dog treats and peanuts to bestow on the animals along her circuit. She even had a male cardinal that kept her company when she worked in her garden. She called him Red Bird. He was around her for about seven years.

The one animal she genuinely feared was a horse. When she was little, mind you, she spent summers on her grandparents' farm in Michigan. She was around horses but steered clear of them. Maybe because they were so big and she was so tiny— I've never been clear about this.

After Mom died, as things were being brought to my house from the lake house so a new family could move in, some long-forgotten treasures turned up. Notably, a limited edition, signed poster of a horse; not just any horse, but Secretariat.

After we visited Churchill Downs on a family vacation many years ago, Mom always made it a yearly event to watch the Kentucky Derby on television. In 1973, a three-year-old stallion won the Derby by two and a half lengths. Mom phoned after the race.

"Did you *see* that?" She was as excited as if she had been present at the rail. "He was so *beautiful!*" I had not seen the race, but I certainly received a complete description of it lasting far longer than the race itself.

Mom was primed for the Preakness. Once again Secretariat won by two and a half lengths. Mom was besotted with this horse. She began collecting and saving articles from newspapers and magazines that told his story. Her telephone conversations were all about this spectacular horse! By then *everyone* who knew anything about horses and horse racing was preparing with great anticipation for the Belmont Stakes. Would he go all the way? Would he win the Triple Crown?

I have to admit, I watched that race, and it was breathtaking. Secretariat won by thirty-one lengths, a true one-horse race. One and a half miles in two minutes and twenty-four seconds, which set a new world record. Sports broadcaster Jim McKay said, "No matter how many times you see that race, it almost takes your breath away." Mom spoke of little else . . . for weeks.

Mom knew where Secretariat was and how he was. She could tell me all about his diet, his personality, and his behaviors. She knew where he was stabled. She knew all about who owned him. She had researched everything she could. And this was in the days before internet search engines. She bought books, magazines, and memorabilia.

In December 1973, my dad's special Christmas gift to my mother was a road trip to Claiborne Farm near Paris, Kentucky. In all the years of their lives together, I think this is the first time Dad came through with an over-the-top surprise that left her reeling. She got to meet Secretariat!

Mom completely forgot she was afraid of horses. She marched right up to the fence that separated her from this glorious stallion. The fence was as tall as my mother. Sensing the total adoration radiating from this little woman from Ohio, Secretariat walked up to the fence and put his magnificent head over it for her to touch his muzzle. He looked her right in the eye. Mom was beyond thrilled.

She had her moment. She petted his muzzle and talked to him as if it were the most normal thing in the world for her to do. Dad snapped a photo of her with her face inches away from Secretariat's eyes. It was her dream come true.

For the rest of Secretariat's life, Mom continued to collect articles about him whenever new information was published. The signed poster went up in her bedroom in a place of honor near photos of her grandchildren. In 1989, Secretariat was suffering from a painful hoof disease. He was put down humanely that year and buried in a six foot by six foot casket lined with silk. Mom was heartbroken.

My mother made the trip to Claiborne Farm one more time. This time she took her father with her. Together they left a large bouquet of red roses on Secretariat's grave. She photographed the headstone.

In her home by the lake, Mom put up a little shrine to Secretariat. The photo of her with him taken years before was put in a frame along with the photo of the headstone and roses.

Which brings me back to the boxes in the basement. I finally have the emotional strength necessary to sort through the things that made up the trail of my mother's life—her journals, photos, scrapbooks, favorite hymnals, and her Secretariat memorabilia. Some things can easily be released to new homes. But there is something about the connection my mother forged with a beautiful horse . . . a horse who took her beyond her fears.

I'm sitting here among the things that meant so much to her, and I've placed the photo of Mom and Secretariat on my desk. I can still hear her voice and the excitement in it whenever she spoke of Secretariat. "He's *magnificent!* I don't know what it is, but I just love him. I can't explain it . . ."

Finding a way to pay honor and tribute to this extraordinary aspect of my mother's life is only just now coming to me.

I have a tiny amount of my mother's ashes left. It's time for me to make the trip to Claiborne Farm. I can think of no greater way to honor my mother than to take some red roses to Secretariat's resting place and set the last of her ashes on the wind over Claiborne Farm. Rest well . . . both of you.

44 tat he

Black Jack, the Riderless Horse

The last of the Army Quartermaster-issued horses with the U.S. brand was Black Jack, named for General John Pershing. The horse was most famous for his role in the funeral procession for President John F. Kennedy. Black Jack served as the caparisoned horse. He was led in the procession, fully saddled, with riderless boots reversed in the stirrups to honor the fallen, as per Army tradition.

In his retirement at the stables of the Caisson Platoon, 1st Battalion, 3rd Infantry, Fort Myer, Virginia, Black Jack enjoyed National Treasure status. School children were frequent, attentive visitors. His birthday was marked each year with a party and visitors from all over the country.

Upon his death, Black Jack received full military honors when his cremains were interred at the edge of Summerall Field parade grounds, Fort Myer, Virginia.

—Claudia Wolfe St. Clair

Rocky

Wanda Dyson

When my husband, Jim, wanted to move us from the suburbs to the country, he knew he'd have to bribe me. And he knew the perfect bribe to use. He promised me I could have a horse.

I was raised on stories of Black Beauty and Flicka and Misty of Chincoteague. I collected Breyer horses, had horse posters on my wall, and dreamed of riding across open fields on my own horse. So the idea of a house with land and a barn and a tack room kick-started some old dreams and started my planning for horses.

After we moved into our "farmette," Jim decided to surprise me by purchasing a pretty little Appaloosa mare at a horse auction. She was surefooted and sweet and extremely well trained. And she barely tolerated me. Springtime Lady was firmly and completely in love with Jim. When I rode her, she would wait until we were about a mile from home and pretend to limp. I'd get off to check it out, and she'd run home. So after she left me to walk home for the third time, I raised the white flag, gave her to Jim, and went back to horse hunting.

I looked at several horses, but none seemed right to me. I finally found an ad for a horse who sounded good. I'd already found that ads could be deceiving, but I gave the owner a call and drove nearly an hour away to see this horse. And fell instantly in love.

His name was Rocket, but everyone called him Rocky. He was a chestnut Arabian—high spirited, regal, and proudly aloof. And he was smarter than most of his riders, including me that first year. My adventures with horses began.

Jim and I took snow rides on our horses, when the world is so quiet you can hear your heart beat. In the spring we'd pack up lunches and do all-day trail rides through the Gettysburg battlefield, seeing parts of that field no tourist ever sees. We'd race across unplowed fields, meander through the woods, and swim the horses in the river. The world looks so different from the back of a horse. I learned to appreciate it in ways I never thought possible.

Soon Lady and Rocky were joined by several more horses. I found out the fat man at the local horse auction was the "meat man" and that he bought cheap horses, even if they were perfectly good trail horses, and hauled them off to slaughter. I couldn't stand the thought of it, so Jim and I started "rescuing" some of these horses. Some we kept; some we put a little work into and sold.

Rocky

When family members came to ride, I'd start the beginners out on Rocky. Not because he was the calmest. Not because he was the gentlest. But because I knew he'd take care of those riders. When my eight-year-old nephew, Lee, wanted to learn to ride, I put him on Rocky and took him into the pasture. I explained to Lee how to find his seat, how to use his legs, how to sit, how to relax, and how to make the horse turn. When I told Lee to turn right and Lee pulled to the left, Rocky turned right. He knew his left from his right even if my nephew did not! But Lee soon had the confidence to get on one of the trail horses and go out on a ride with the adults.

As the herd increased from two to four, then six, then seven, the pecking order shifted. But Rocky always remained the alpha male, and Lady always remained alpha female. Any horses who came in thinking they could mosey up to the first two food bowls at feeding time soon regretted that idea and slunk off sporting a nip or kick.

Even so, feeding time in the corral could be dangerous. Jim and I finally stopped walking around inside the corral filling feed bowls and bought bowls we could hang on the fence. Then we'd walk down the safe side of the fence to feed the horses.

When our daughter, Jayme, was about three years old, we tried putting her on a horse and walking her around. But she simply never fell in love with horses. We bought her a pony, thinking maybe the sheer size of an eight-hundred-pound horse bothered her. She rejected them all. She loved animals but preferred dogs, cats, and rabbits. Sometimes she'd come out to the barn and watch as we brushed the horses or had them in the training ring, but she would sit on the grass in the yard and watch from a safe distance.

But on one fateful day, she broke all the rules. And Rocky proved there was more to a horse than good looks.

Jim and I were walking the fence line, dumping grain into the feeding bowls. The horses were making their usual fuss and fight over position, shifting and nipping, with even the occasional kick. I was almost to the last bowl when I noticed Rocky was standing in the middle of the paddock area, ignoring the food bowls. His ears lay flat and his teeth were bared.

I walked back up the fence line and then heard my husband scream out my daughter's name. I ran. But she wasn't sitting on the grass. She was in the middle of the paddock. The little minx had realized there was a huge tub of water, and she wanted her Barbie doll to go for a swim. Oblivious to the danger, she was happily dunking her doll in the water and giggling.

But what made my heart start beating again was that Rocky was standing over her, making sure no other horse came near her. If she moved, he moved—ever keeping her right beneath him so he could protect her. If another horse came close, he'd flatten his ears and kick out a warning.

Jim managed to clear a path for me to get to Rocky and Jayme. I pulled my daughter out from under Rocky and carried her out of the paddock, safe and sound. There was not a scratch on her. Then I gave Rocky an extra portion of grain because someone had slipped over and eaten his dinner while he protected Jayme.

I never looked at a horse the same way again. Sure, some of the horses we had over the years were blockheads, but even then, we found something special in each one. Kris loved to steal hats off people and run away with them. Nanza took a blind horse under her wing and would lead him all over the property.

If he wandered too far from her, Nanza would whinny shrilly until he returned. Austin, our gentle giant, couldn't stand to be ridden in a confined space. Bonnie hated going in deep water, and Lady loved it.

And Rocky? He's now thirty-five years old and lives out his comfortable and pampered retirement on my sister's farm in North Carolina.

The Girl Who Read to Horses

Gwen Ellis

It was midnight when the phone rang, and I hurried to answer it. I had just returned from the urgent care center, where my daughter-in-law, Chandra, had taken my five-year-old granddaughter, Paige, for treatment of what we thought was a bladder infection. My daughter, Wendy, and I had accompanied Chandra and Paige to the urgent care center, but as the hour grew late, I went home.

"Mom," Chandra said on the phone, "we have a problem. Paige has Type 1 [juvenile] diabetes and we are headed straight to the hospital."

What? Stop the world! Not my beautiful, blue-eyed, dark-haired, smart-as-a-whip granddaughter. *No, God, no!*

"Would you go to the house and stay with the baby so Mark can meet me at the hospital?"

Of course I would, and in a short time, my distraught son opened the door to let me into their apartment. Emotion spilled out of me. "Oh, Mark, no. Not our Paigey. This can't be happening." But it was, and the freight train of fear and despair thundered toward us.

Early the next morning Mark burst into the apartment and said Paige was being transferred by ambulance to Santa Barbara Children's Hospital immediately. Almost as soon as he came, he was gone. Later in the morning, after I had fed and dressed baby John, I strapped him into his car seat, and we drove to the hospital. I pushed his stroller into the elevator, down the hall, and into Paige's room. There she sat, a tiny five-year-old child lost in a huge hospital bed in the pediatric intensive care unit.

Paige was the kind of child who spoke early, used big words, and talked endlessly. You could give her a bath and she never stopped talking. You could serve her dinner and she kept talking. You could strap her into a car seat and her motor mouth kept running. She talked and talked and talked about everything and nothing. But this morning she was very quiet. She looked up, smiled, and said, "Hi, Grammy," and that was about all.

After almost a week in intensive care, Paige was stable, and we took her home. If you think taking a newborn home from the hospital when you have no experience as a parent is frightening, then try taking home a diabetic child whose life depends on each decision you make for her. We weren't sure we knew enough to adequately manage the disease. But we had no choice; we had to learn and learn quickly.

Paige truly is more advanced than the average child her age, and in no time at all she could talk with her doctors about her pancreas and beta cells and glucose and insulin and how they all work together. She knew what was happening to her, and in some ways that made it easier to deal with her needs.

After a while it was time to deal with the emotional fallout Paige might experience from this change in her life. About this time Wendy heard that a horse rescue in the area was bringing its mascot rescue horse, a Shetland named Taffy, to the library to meet the kids. She thought it might be therapeutic for Paige to meet this pony who had suffered hurt and was now thriving. Within a few days, not only did Paige meet Taffy, but Chandra had arranged for her to visit the rescue facility out in the hills near Ojai, California. There she would meet horses who, through no fault of their own, were neglected or injured or sick—just like Paige.

Paige took to the idea like a duck to water. Of course, looking through the fence at the twenty or so horses was great, but she wanted to get into the stalls and muck them out and groom the horses and feed them and do everything involved in horse care. She understood hurt, and she wanted to help those animals who stood three times as tall as she was to get over what they had endured. She cared.

"Paige, I know you want to help," the attendant told her, "but we can't let you into the horses' stalls. You are still too little. You'll have to wait until you are eight."

Paige thought about the situation. Then she came up with a solution that worked for everyone. "I'll read to them," she said.

Eyes popped open at that. No one had ever suggested reading to the animals. The staff agreed that she could put a chair outside the corral fence and sit and read. I doubt they were prepared for what happened next.

Paige had learned to read well by the time she was three and could read rather lengthy chapter books by the age of five. But for the horses, she didn't choose the long books. Instead she went back to picture books like *Good Night Moon* and *The Cat in the Hat* and her other favorites.

Most Saturdays found Paige sitting outside the pens with her favorite books in her lap, reading aloud. The horses pressed close to the corral fence, then poked their heads through the railings and touched her knee with their soft noses. They just touched her—reached out to her—letting her know that she and they were going to be okay.

Those horses quickly fell in love with this little person who sat quietly and read to them. And one of the first horses to respond to her was a magnificent animal named Cheyenne. Cheyenne had suffered more than any other horse at the rescue operation. He didn't trust anyone, but slowly, ever so slowly, he began to accept carrots from Paige's hand. When he heard her chipper little voice across the paddock fences, his head would come up and his ears would move toward her voice.

Two and a half years passed, and finally Paige was eight. Now she could muck the stalls, learn to brush and curry the horses, and even learn to use a pick on their feet to remove stones. She put together a little tack box of her own that she took to the rescue with her. She learned to ride and lost all fear of the animals who towered over her. When one of the horses, a pregnant mare who was rescued from the slaughter house the day she was to be killed, gave birth to a beautiful little red colt named Jasper, Paige was enchanted; even when that rascal Jasper started stealing her hat or trying to nip her to get attention, Paige took it all in stride. Busy in the stalls, interacting with and caring for the animals, she didn't read to them as often as she had before, but the relationship had been forged and the animals accepted her moving around them.

From the day she was born, Paige has loved animals of all kinds. And somewhere deep inside her she has understanding and concern for all animals. But it is horses she loves the most. We are deeply grateful for her time spent with those animals and for the workers at the horse rescue who allowed a little girl to participate in the best way she knew how—by becoming the girl who read to horses.

When "Hi-Ho" Silver Came to Our House

Lauraine Snelling

"We got a horse!"

I announced it to all of the kids in our neighborhood, if you could call the collection of small farms along Old Frontier Road a neighborhood. I started broadcasting the news when I got on the school bus Monday morning, and by the time I got off the bus that afternoon everyone was planning on coming to meet Silver. Someone finally had a horse!

I had dreamed of having another horse of my own ever since my pony, Polly, died the last winter we lived in Minnesota. We moved to Washington State the summer I was ten, but in town with no place for a horse. It was a few years before Mom and Dad got the opportunity to farm again, and I was that much closer to my "someday" horse.

Ecstatic does not begin to cover my joy and jumping-up-and-down delight when a white horse backed out of the trailer onto our driveway. His name was Silver. While he didn't have the stature of Silver of *The Lone Ranger* movies, he was mine, or rather he belonged to all three of us—my younger sister, brother, and me.

But I was *the* horse lover.

My brother, Don, and I rode Silver around the pasture later that afternoon with a bridle but no saddle. Since my sister, Karen, was only six, I led her around with a lead rope. Basking in the thrill of having a horse again, the three of us all learned how to stay on and guide him with the reins, since he was trained western style.

Silver seemed friendly, enjoying the attention as I brushed him, combed out his tail, checked hooves, kissed his nose, and inhaled the oh-so-wonderful fragrance of horse. How I had missed that.

While Silver's hair was all white, his skin was dark in places, white in others, and pink with dark freckles around his muzzle. From the way he arched his neck and carried his head and tail, he looked to be part Arabian. He enjoyed munching on chunks of carrot and oats. He even crunched a hard peppermint candy, then spread his lips wide and shook his head, making me laugh.

I laughed a lot that day, out of sheer joy. I had a horse again. I could hardly wait until my friends met Silver. I knew for certain he would become my best friend. And we'd have many adventures because we lived near miles of logging roads left over from a once vibrant timber industry.

When I let Silver out in the pasture after all his attention, I leaned on the gate, watching him drop to his knees and roll, feet kicking in the air. He got up, shook himself, dust flying, and ambled off, nibbling the ankle-deep grass and acquainting himself with his new territory. In tune with his antics, my whole body thrummed with a when-can-I-ride-him-again rhythm.

Fast forward to Monday. I could hardly sit still all day during class. A horse. I had a horse at home. I drew horses on my notebook, wrote Silver ten different ways in the margins, and got caught passing a note to my best friend.

The teacher read it aloud. "You're coming, aren't you?" He stared at me. "Are you inviting all of us then? And to what, may I ask, are we coming?"

Death by embarrassment was a real fear for this young girl. Or a wish at that point. I spoke to my desk. "To see my new horse."

He heaved a long-suffering sigh. "You realize there are a lot of blackboards that need washing and erasers cleaned?"

Eyes glued shut, I pleaded silently, *Please don't make me stay after school. Please don't. I'll do the chores for a week if you just let me go home on time today.* The walk home was a long mile, and no one would be there to come pick me up. Besides, I knew that if someone were there, they would not come pick me up for a reason such as this. You paid your penalties yourself. My dad would say, "The walk will give you plenty of time to think about not passing notes again."

Back to the classroom. "Since this is your first offense, you are excused. But should I catch you passing notes again, young lady, the penalty will be double."

"Yes, sir, thank you, sir." Relief melted me into the seat.

School finally let out. Ten kids from the young age of six to my twelve promised they'd be at our house as soon as they could get there. I changed out of my school clothes in record speed, grabbed something to eat, and, joined by my two siblings, headed for the barn.

From the grain bin I retrieved a can with enough oats on the bottom to rattle well, and the three of us went to the fence. All the while I dreamed of my horse trotting up to the fence when I whistled, although I reminded myself that Silver had yet to learn to respond to my whistle. After all my friends arrived, I practiced whistling and shook the oats in the coffee can.

"Come on, Silver, at least raise your head and notice us." I opened the gate and all of us trooped through. My dad had warned me to make sure I closed the gate, so I did, making doubly sure the wire loop fit snugly over the post.

Our six acres of pastures were divided by several fences, and Silver had chosen to graze in the largest one. We all walked through a usually left-open gate to where the horse grazed, albeit now with head up, watching our approach. I rattled the oats, calling, "Come, Silver. Come meet your friends."

The horse just stood there, tail swishing flies, ears flicking back and forth. Silver was not a big horse, about 14.2 hands, which would make it easier for us kids to mount him. The day before I had tried grabbing a piece of mane and swinging aboard him like riders on TV did. Let's just say the actors sure make it look a lot easier than it is. I did manage to mount with a running leap, however, and landed belly-flat against Silver's backbone. He'd not tried to get away, although someone was holding his reins at the time, just in case.

As our group drew closer, I shook the oat can more enticingly and called out to him in my most winsome tone. "Easy, fellah. Come on now. Meet your new friends." He was so beautiful, all white against the green field. Had I buttons on my T-shirt, they would have popped for sure. I had a horse again. Love bloomed the whole scene rosy. Less brave than the others, Karen kept herself slightly behind me while the other children hung together, laughing and poking each other in anticipation.

"He's just like Silver on the TV!" That was a comment that made me warm all over.

"Come on, boy. You like oats. I know you do." If only he would come to me. That's what horses were supposed to do, at least in books and movies they always did, and I'd read or watched every one that existed. "Come on, Silver." I rattled and shook the oat can.

The group was about ten feet away, laughing and chattering, when Silver pinned both ears flat to his head, bared his teeth, and charged! Oats and can flew up in the air. My heart leaped out of my chest. Everyone screamed and ran. Surely that fence, behind which safety dwelled, couldn't be a mile away. It was every kid for himself. I'm sure I was yelling, "Hurry! Faster!" Or did I need all my air just to run?

You have never seen ten kids run for a fence and get through it or roll under three strands of barbed wire in so little time, and yet it all felt like it was happening in slow motion. From the other side of the fence, we were all puffing and panting, sure that the fierce and vicious horse was right on our heels, ready to pummel us into the grass. But when we looked back, Silver was in about the same spot, placidly grazing on the spilled oats.

Oh, no, I have a mean horse. How could he act like this? He'd been so good the day before. I checked everyone over. No horse bites, only two barbed wire scratches, and a couple of ripped shirts. For some odd reason no one wanted to go with me to meet Silver again, not that I wanted to either, but I had to save face somehow.

Needless to say, no one rode that day. No one petted my horse. Our family now had a pasture ornament. At least he kept the field grazed.

Over the next few months, I tried every way to catch that horse, but every time I tried to brave his charge-out, when he got close enough to me, he'd spin and raise his back hooves like he was going to kick me clear over the barn. Had I known how to throw a lasso, I would have caught him with that. He ate hay with the cows and enjoyed his life of leisure through the months of fall until our first snowfall. Quickly his hooves packed with snow, and he was forced to hobble around.

I knew I had to help him. He was my horse, my best friend, even if he didn't know it yet. We had adventures to experience. But how? Don and I herded him into a smaller pen. With a rope attached to the halter and the halter draped over my arm, I walked up to him. My heart near to plugged my throat; blood hammered in my ears. I kept saying to myself, *Lauraine, you have to help him. He's your horse whether he wants to be or not.*

Silver laid back his ears. I kept talking to him. He stumbled, spinning to kick toward me. Instead of obeying my common sense that said to *get out of there*, I laid a hand on his rump, the first time I had touched him since that miserable Monday. He didn't kick. He didn't bite. His ears went forward, and he turned his head to look at me over his shoulder.

What in the world? What happened? Moving one hand along his back, I made my way toward his head, slid the rope around his neck, and after buckling the halter in place and cooing at him all the while, I fed him a handful of oats from the can Don handed to me. I then tied him to the board fence and cleaned the ice out of his poor hooves. I nearly slithered down the fence to the snowy ground. I had caught Silver. That horse had buf-faloed me for three months.

All I needed to do was put a hand on him, and he settled right down. Eventually my family and I learned that even twine was enough rope for him to figure he was caught. From then on, we used a long length of twine to corral him into a corner, put a hand on him, and wait a moment for him to relax. He never, ever kicked or bit any of us. He also never came when called or whistled to. And usually, catching him was a two man—er, kid—operation.

But my training *by* Silver was just beginning. When weather permitted, I rode him all around our pastures and out on the miles of logging roads, finally experiencing those many adventures I had dreamed about. I came to believe that he would not take me where it was not safe to go, such as muddy, swampy areas, through low-hanging branches, into deep brush, or near other animals that might be dangerous. I had to trust Silver like he trusted me.

He also taught me about changing leads—or dancing as I called it— playing broom and basketball polo, and how to make him rear, just like the real "Hi-Ho" Silver. The first time I rode him in a community parade, when the high school band began to play, Silver strutted to the music. When the band turned and marched the other way, so did we. Later my family learned Silver had been owned by a military officer at one time, who had indeed ridden him in parades.

Through the years I learned to trust Silver, not only with myself but with non-riders as well. I watched him shift to the side when a small child was on his back and in danger of sliding off. He always walked carefully, more like a mule than a horse.

I eventually traded a Jersey heifer that wouldn't breed for a Saddlebred Morgan mare named Kit, which began a whole new chapter of horse adventures. Silver kept on training my brother and sister, cousins, friends, and all those we brought his way. After I left home for college, and Don and Karen weren't riding any longer, our folks gave Silver to a family down the road with small children so he could keep on training new kids.

God has been teaching me about trust my whole life, to trust in him and to trust in others. That time he used a white horse named Silver to teach me that one must have the guts to look beyond the bluster, the hostile body language, and the masks we all wear from time to time, to reach out and uncover the heart buried there. Trust means giving up control. With just a touch of my hand on his rump, Silver gave up his control to me. He trusted me to feed him, care for him, and protect him. He trusted that by doing so his reward would be great.

So starting then, continuing today and most probably for the rest of my life, I am learning to give control of my life to my heavenly Father. Now, that takes a lot of trust, but he never gives up, not like I wanted to with that white horse of so many years ago. And I am forever grateful I didn't.

Macaroni, the White House Pony

The JFK White House was the first to have preschool children romping about. Both Jack and Jackie Kennedy were animal lovers, and consequently the White House menagerie consisted of dogs, rabbits, hamsters, goldfish, parakeets, a canary, ducks, deer, and a pony who had his run of the White House lawn. The round, good-natured pony was named Macaroni, and he was much-photographed. He was known to chomp away at the red roses in the famous Rose Garden, and tourists fed the chunky little guy through the fence so much that chicken wire had to be put up to stop them.[4]

A Friend Who Sticks Closer than a Brother

Catherine Ulrich Brakefield

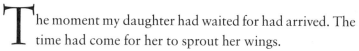

The moment my daughter had waited for had arrived. The time had come for her to sprout her wings.

Nothing came easy for Kimberly. But she was resolute and a true-blue friend to her handful of school chums, and even though the girls in the popular set in school were her constant critics, she gaily joined the cheerleading squad.

She immediately felt the chasm between herself and the "in crowd" widen.

My husband, Edward, and I weren't sure what to do. Then we purchased a 15-hand high, chocolate-colored mare named Candy. My fourteen-year-old daughter had taken English riding lessons and had been riding since she was eight years old. She was elated when she learned Candy was to be her new horse.

It wasn't long, however, before I saw a side of Candy that made me uncomfortable. Candy could be sweet but stubborn. During riding lessons Candy did not hesitate to take advantage of Kimberly whenever she let her guard down. Candy would throw her neck down to the ground if she did not want to trot or canter and unseat my daughter.

In human terms, Candy was a bully. She could give Kimberly's human tormenters a few pointers. Candy knew her strength and took advantage of a less-experienced and weaker rider.

I was ready to try my daughter on another mount. My thoughts went to the four-year-old dapple gray gelding Edward and I were just finishing up training.

Baja was a straight-line-bred Crabbet Arabian. Edward and I had purchased him when he was a teary-eyed three-month-old weanling. His mother had been re-bred and consequently Baja was separated from her early. I doted on him that first year. He had come to trust Edward and me over the biting and kicking horses that were determined to show him his place in the pecking order of life.

Now, at four years, Baja couldn't care less if you were straddling him or walking alongside him. He had the type of temperament horse people dream of. He was people-oriented. He loved to be handled, liked to be doted on, and didn't care what you did with him just as long as you were doing it with him.

My husband and I had completed the arena work and now cantered Baja across hay fields and meadows. Never in Baja's training did he buck or rear. He did an occasional shy, but that didn't amount to anything more than a side step. Needless to say, Edward claimed him immediately.

My concerns about Candy grew. I decided to ride her while Edward took out a young Arabian mare named Miriah for a cross-country ride. Cantering along one of our trails, we decided to take the fork through a dense growth of underbrush. A flock of pheasants flew up, and Candy's front feet pawed the air in a full rear. Miriah, startled, backed up and stared at Candy. That was it. I didn't want my daughter on this horse.

But Kimberly had become attached to Candy. "She's my horse, Mom. She likes me." Kimberly continued to persist, explaining that Candy was as tired as she was of the indoor arena. She would be fine riding Candy cross-country.

I realized Candy had healed the place in my daughter's heart the girls at school had bruised. Kimberly, being a true-blue friend, could not let her horse down.

I could not hold back the inevitable. Saddling up that morning, I wondered what this obstinate mare would do when presented with the opportunity to gallop across the wide-open spaces with a small girl straddling her ample middle. I didn't have long to find out. Halfway down the lane, Candy did a half rear and bolted forward. Candy didn't care to go far; she just wanted to unseat and scare my daughter.

Kimberly did exceptionally well. She gathered her reins, turned the now-trotting horse into a tight circle, and stopped her.

But big wet tears dripped down her cheeks as Kimberly removed Candy's bridle and saddle. "Mom, I don't ever want to ride again."

I wrapped my arms around her quivering shoulders. If I did not get her back on a horse, I wasn't sure she would ever want to ride. Candy had been her confidante, her friend, and her partner against the unfairness of life. Now that friendship had turned into a carbon copy of what she'd experienced with her schoolmates: rejection.

There was one alternative left for me to pursue.

"Pick up your saddle."

"Why? Didn't you hear me? I'm through. And I'm through with cheerleading too!"

I walked down the aisle and opened Baja's stall, stroked his head, and whispered, "Okay, boy, it's all up to you. I know you can do it."

Kimberly scowled up at Baja. "I don't think so."

"I know so." I grabbed my daughter's saddle and plopped it onto Baja's back.

We were off. No arena work, no preliminaries. We were cantering down the same hay field where Candy had acted up with my daughter. Baja did his slow rocking-chair canter with Kimberly, and my horse cantered alongside. We came to the bend in the field and started to walk around the coup, a wooden three-foot-high jump. Suddenly a flock of blackbirds flew up in front of Baja's face. He started to sidestep. Kimberly, totally surprised, was thrown sideways on him. Baja stopped, trembling. Kimberly straightened herself, and Baja continued his shy.

"Good, Baja." Kimberly ran her hands down Baja's neck. Baja nickered, as if to say, "Yeah, that was scary."

"Well, I guess I will have to be the one to tell your dad that he just lost his favorite horse."

Kimberly's broad smile confirmed my words.

This began a love affair that continued on through 4-H, fox hunt rides, and distance riding competitions. The years sped by, friends came and went for Kimberly, and always there was her faithful Baja. Kimberly's self-confidence grew and so did her popularity. When Kimberly married, the first thing packed up to go to her new home was Baja. In three short years Baja had his work cut out for him, teaching Kimberly's two sons how to ride.

Sadly, nothing in life remains like we want it.

The day started out like any other. The warm, autumn breezes swept the grassy meadow gently. This was the day Baja quietly lay down amid the sweet-smelling pastures of his home for the last time. Now the ripe old age of twenty-seven, Baja, being the gentleman he was, graciously said his good-byes with his doting family members petting him farewell. Kimberly wrapped her arms around his neck and sobbed her good-bye into his ear. The words of Matthew 25:21 came wafting into my mind: "Well done, good and faithful servant."

Baja had been there for my daughter. I could have asked for no more than this. Throughout Kimberly's trying teen years, Baja was a true-blue friend who stuck closer than a brother. He gave my daughter the courage she needed to sprout her wings of confidence. God had provided my daughter the perfect friend when she needed one.

Paintbrushes and
Horse Cookies

Susy Flory

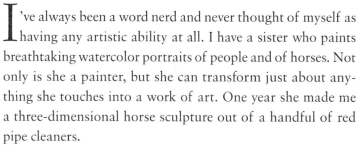

I've always been a word nerd and never thought of myself as having any artistic ability at all. I have a sister who paints breathtaking watercolor portraits of people and of horses. Not only is she a painter, but she can transform just about anything she touches into a work of art. One year she made me a three-dimensional horse sculpture out of a handful of red pipe cleaners.

I can barely draw a straight line, and the best I could do was draw stick figures that always looked like crooked balloons with spider legs. But in my twenties I started working a retail job at a mall store called Stamp-a-teria that sold rubber stamps and supplies. There I discovered you don't have to know how to draw to use a rubber stamp. Something deep inside unlocked, and for the first time in my life I felt like I could be creative too.

I chose my stamps carefully and added vivid colors with markers, pencils, and glitter glue. There were no rules, and I found myself captivated by the journey of discovering what each little stamped art piece wanted to be and learning to have faith in the process—because sometimes what happens along the way is, after all, the point.

That's what happened with an artist I met recently. His name is Metro, and he was discovered by the local newspaper in his hometown of Gettysburg, Pennsylvania. The TV station in Harrisburg picked up the story; then the Fox morning show in Baltimore did. Before long *The Today Show* did a feature, and Metro's colorful abstract paintings began selling at a local art gallery. The gallery started a waiting list, and soon over a hundred people were dying for a Metro original. Every painting sold within seconds.

But Metro doesn't care much about the money or the fame. As long as he gets his hay, he's happy, because Metro is a horse.

A tall, athletic thoroughbred, Metro raced at Belmont Park and won over $300,000 in his three-year career. But when he developed bone chips in his knees, the horse was quickly retired and adopted by a shy man named Ron, who knew next to nothing about horses.

Metro was a difficult horse, cranky and stubborn, even biting and kicking when he was in a bad mood. But Ron stuck with him; something about the retired racehorse captivated Ron, even though experienced trainers and stable owners branded Metro dangerous, warning Ron that the horse had no future. During one grooming session, Metro savagely bit Ron's wife on the thigh. She burst into tears, and the massive bruise was sore for days. But she refused to give up on Metro, and so did Ron. "Metro is like our child," explained Ron. "He's the first thing I think about in the morning and the last thing I think about when I go to bed."

With extensive training, using natural horsemanship techniques like those developed by horse whisperers such as Clinton Anderson and Buck Brannaman, Ron was finally able to get Metro to the point where he could take him out on trail rides. His hard work and the money, time, and emotion he had invested were finally beginning to pay off. Then Ron noticed Metro was developing a limp. He knew training for the racetrack is very hard on the body of a young horse, and the damage is sometimes irreversible. The news from the vet wasn't good. "His riding days are over," the vet said after reading the X-rays. "Metro has about two years before his knees completely lock up." Ron's heart sank.

"What about surgery?" Ron asked. The vet explained that since Metro had already been through two knee surgeries early in his career, there wasn't enough healthy bone left, and surgery was not an option. They'd already tried supplements. The vet did suggest a last-ditch treatment—an experimental set of injections had shown some promise in Europe, but Ron didn't have that kind of money.

Finally, after much discussion, the vet said those words Ron had been dreading. "When his knees lock up, Metro will need to be euthanized."

Ron was in instant agony, his mind racing as he searched for an idea, a solution, a way out of this nightmare. Then a crazy thought popped into his head, and out of his mouth.

"Can he paint?" Ron was pretty sure the vet had never heard that question before.

"What? Paint?"

"Yes, stand in front of a canvas and hold a paintbrush in his mouth."

The vet took a moment or two to answer, then stammered, "I-I imagine so."

Ron had been making his living painting pet portraits, mostly dogs, and thinking about this idea for a while. While Ron felt uncomfortable around people, he loved being in front of a blank canvas, and he thought that feeling of being at home might just transmit to Metro. Also, the horse was a quick learner. He'd come off the track with an unruly personality and a definite lack of manners, but over the years he'd learned how to behave, at least most of the time. Painting was an activity the two could do together that wouldn't hurt Metro's knees; he would be comfortably standing still with no weight on his back.

Then there was the head bobbing. From the very first day Metro came off the track, Ron had watched him bob his head up and down. For some horses, it seems to be a nervous condition, but when Metro peered out over the stall door and flung his head up and down, Ron knew he was bored and trying to get attention. Either that or he was protesting about something. Ron had the feeling if he could get Metro to hold a paintbrush in his teeth, he could teach him how to stroke the brush across a canvas. He wasn't at all sure it would work, but he couldn't wait to try. If Metro only had two years left, the time to start was now.

While Metro had proved himself a quick learner in the past, he didn't like to do anything twice. So Ron kept the first few art lessons short. He strapped a blank canvas securely to an easel, weighted so it couldn't be easily tipped over. Next Ron brought in an ample supply of Metro's favorite horse cookies, made of molasses and oats. Last, he decided to keep the painting lessons to just ten minutes a day. Within a week, Metro learned to hold a dry paintbrush in his mouth and touch it to the canvas.

Next it was time to introduce paint. Ron squeezed out some non-toxic acrylic paints onto a tray, dipped the brush into the paint, and handed it to Metro. *Will he make strokes?* Ron had no idea how to teach him to move his big head and make strokes on the canvas. Metro would have to do that on his own. Another worry galloped through Ron's mind. *Will Metro have the patience to hold the brush or will he get distracted and drop it?* If so, that could be the end of Ron's dream of making paintings with his horse. He didn't have a back-up plan.

But when he handed Metro the brush, the horse gripped it in his mouth, just like they had practiced, and turned to the canvas, stroking paint across it. As Ron watched Metro stroke the paint onto canvas, his eyes filled with tears. *My horse is amazing. Does he know horses don't do this? Is he embracing this? Could making paintings be his destiny?*

Nothing with Metro had been easy, but somehow teaching him to paint was effortless. Ron chose the colors, dipped the brush in the paint, and Metro did the rest, joyfully stroking the brush up and down and across the canvas. Within months, Metro and Ron were turning out colorful abstract paintings with bold strokes of complementary colors, and they flew off the walls of the local art gallery. Ron decided to use the money to try the experimental European knee injections. To his delight, the treatment worked. Metro would live—and paint—much longer than two years. The activity Ron came up with to enrich Metro's last years turned out to be the very thing that saved his life. And now Metro's paintings are saving other horses off the track with the profits going to rehabilitate other racehorses in need.

Some have questioned whether Metro's colorful canvases can be considered art. Those same critics would probably say the same about my rubber stamp creations. But Metro's paintings are art—the art of dance, with Ron and Metro anticipating each other's every move. The art of communication, with two artists talking though no words are exchanged. And the art of teamwork, with man and horse together creating something where before there was nothing.

Thomas Merton said, "Art enables us to find ourselves and lose ourselves at the same time."[5] If that is true, Ron and Metro find themselves a little more each time Metro bobs his head up and down and picks up a paintbrush bathed in bright colors.

Yours for a Year

Sarah Dowlearn

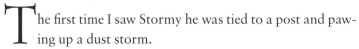

The first time I saw Stormy he was tied to a post and pawing up a dust storm.

The September afternoon was brisk but not cold. I had just started my junior year of high school, and though a pile of homework awaited me, I drove to the barn as soon as school got out. I didn't recognize the chestnut Arabian gelding who was making a ruckus, whinnying and swinging his haunches back and forth. He didn't make a great first impression.

Terry, my riding instructor and the barn owner, appeared from the doorway of the barn, smashing her worn hat down over short white hair and wiping her hands on faded blue jeans. I waved.

"Who's the new horse?"

"That's Stormy. Somebody just gave him to me. He's been sitting in a pasture for six years."

We walked over to where Stormy stood. He had paused his tantrum to watch the horses in the arena, his body tense and alert.

"What are you going to do with him?"

"He's your new project horse. I want you to work with him. He's yours for a year."

I had grown used to Terry's blunt style, but still I choked with surprise. Terry always said it took a year to establish a strong partnership with a horse, but without a horse of my own, I'd never had a chance to test that theory. For five years I'd been honing my skills on sensible, well-trained lesson horses.

"How old is he?"

"Eighteen."

I looked at Stormy again. Eighteen years old? Age had done little to further his education. I reached out to stroke the white blaze on his face. This was going to be a challenge.

It didn't take long for me to realize what I'd been saddled with in working with Stormy. Slow was not in his vocabulary, and I could barely sit his floaty, bouncy trot. To him, leg cues only meant go. And shoulder control? He leaned through turns like a bike careening around a corner. His brakes were hit and miss. He didn't cross water. He spooked at the air. He was so narrow that Terry joked that his front legs came out of the same hole.

As a horse-crazy girl, I didn't think it was possible to dislike a horse. But that first month with Stormy had me reconsidering. After the smooth, well-behaved lesson horses I was used to, Stormy was jarring and stubborn. He'd stick his nose in the air or go fast as I struggled to teach him to respond to my cues. Some days I dismounted wondering if I'd really accomplished anything. I didn't know how to fail. As a perfectionist and a straight-A student, failure was my biggest fear. I wrapped my identity up in my performance. Stormy forced me to face my insecurities, and it was downright uncomfortable.

Winter came, dark and wet, making it difficult for me to work with Stormy. On Wednesday nights I hitched a ride to the barn with some friends, but since we had no covered arena, I spent most of those nights grooming the crusted mud off his coat and doing groundwork in the barn aisle. If I did ride, I had to be careful not to get him too hot and sweaty since it was cold and late. Slowly my feelings toward Stormy thawed.

By springtime Stormy and I had graduated from tolerating each other to a truce. I rode Stormy in my weekly lessons, but most of the time Terry left me to my own devices. She trusted me to try and to fail. And fail I did. Early that spring Stormy and I began to venture out on the trail. This particular day was warm and sunny, and my friend Kelly and I had just started our ride. As we followed the trail traversing a large open field, I looked back over my shoulder.

"Do you want to trot?"

"Sure."

Stormy and I were in the lead, and only a few steps into the trot, I felt his head come up and his body tense. I knew what was coming, but somehow I still wasn't ready when it did. In half a second, he was off the side of the trail, and I was tumbling down into the space he had just vacated. Kelly pulled up her gray mare in time to avoid stepping on me. I picked myself up, unscathed except for a scratch on my pinkie finger. Fortunately, Stormy hadn't gone far, so I picked the star thistle out of my shirt and remounted. To this day, Stormy is the only horse who has managed to dump me on the trail.

Failing wasn't fun, but the process of trial and error taught me more than any of the well-trained lesson horses did. Stormy was forgiving, and little by little, he started to catch on. The better he became, the more I liked him.

Sometimes I had to look for creative approaches to problems. When summer rolled around I was ready to tackle his fear of water. The small pond in the pasture became our training ground. Some of the other horses played in the water of their own accord, but Stormy avoided it like a child who doesn't know how to swim. First I tried lunging him through it, but he veered into the circle to avoid the shallow shore. I tried pressing him forward from the saddle, but he was adamant in his refusal. I tried moving his haunches to step in the water, but he always managed to dance his way out of it.

Then one day I had an unconventional idea. I put on my muck boots, tacked Stormy up in a surcingle and long drive lines, and waded out into the middle of the pond. The green algae lapped against my legs as Stormy pranced at the water's edge. With his tail toward me, I slowly backed him into the pond. When his hooves first touched the water, he startled at the splash, but soon his white stockings disappeared and he was as wet as I was. Once was all it took. From then on Stormy bravely sloshed through streams, ponds, and the nearby lake— no balking or leaping.

I no longer disliked Stormy. In fact, I was getting pretty attached to this copper horse who had come so far and taught me so much.

By fall we were ready to show off what we'd accomplished. The first week of October, just over one year from when we began our journey, Stormy and I participated in the barn's annual schooling show. We did well in some gymkhana and equitation classes, but the trail class represented the pinnacle of our achievement. Stormy calmly ponied another horse, side passed, walked over a bridge, splashed through the pond, traversed up and down a steep incline, and maneuvered a scary tarp obstacle. When the scores were announced, we had earned second place!

I found Terry later that afternoon. She had been busy running the show and was surprised when she heard the news.

"What? Stormy got second? I never would have thought that."

If you had asked me in the beginning, I never would have thought so either. I continued to ride and enjoy my now-beloved Stormy until I went off to college the next year. But I didn't forget him or the lessons I learned. Stormy taught me not to give up, to try and to fail, and to challenge myself.

And that first impressions aren't everything.

Seventeen Horses at Tender Lives Ranch

Robert W. Busha

For seven years my wife, Mary, and I had been crisscrossing the continental United States as Christian missionaries in support of church, parachurch, and community leadership teams. It was May of 2000 and we were in Aztec, New Mexico, near the famous geographical "Four Corners" of New Mexico, Arizona, Utah, and Colorado.

There had been a pattern of sorts in our working and serving. We'd be in an area for three to eighteen months and then be called to another place in the United States. At the time, we were assisting several ministries, but one Friday afternoon I told my wife, "I think I'm supposed to work on a horse ranch in Colorado."

That was unusual for two reasons. First, I didn't know anyone in Colorado with a horse ranch. Second, I'd never worked

100

with horses. The thought persisted, growing stronger. So after church Sunday morning we took a ride in our little red pickup truck north about fifty miles into Colorado.

Because I'd hiked in the mountains of the San Juan National Forest many times, I was aware of a large ranch west of Durango. *Surely*, I thought, *when we drive around that curve on Route 160, there'll be a big "Help Wanted" sign by the highway near the entrance to that ranch*. Disappointment, even a little confusion, swept over me as we went past that ranch and down the grade approaching Mancos. No sign. No helped needed.

We thought we'd salvage the ride and go up the mountain road north of Mancos to a trailhead that has a fantastic view of the peaks and valleys in the San Juan range. Once there, I sat on a bench, appreciating the view of Hesperus Mountain—all 13,232 feet of her—and at that point I apologized to God for my apparent misreading of what I felt certain was his direction for another chapter in our journey. I wondered if, or how, I'd missed it this time.

Back in Aztec, in time for the Sunday evening church service, there was a surprise waiting for us. Assistant Pastor Ron Yepa read a letter he said had been sitting on his desk for about two months. It was from friends of the Aztec church, Pastor Bobby and Carolyn Clement in Colorado. They needed help building a couple of cabins for the young girls who came to their Tender Lives Ranch south of Grand Junction. They hosted weeklong horsemanship camps during the summer months. I instantly knew that invitation was for me. I could drive up and help them for a few weeks.

The next morning, right at nine, I phoned the ranch and explained to Mrs. Clement why I was calling. I had construction experience and felt I was supposed to give them a hand with those cabins. She was a little surprised but told me to call back about noontime when her husband, Bobby, who was harvesting hay with a group of volunteers, would be back for lunch. What she didn't tell me then was they didn't have money at that moment to buy lumber for those cabins.

They told me a few days later that when Carolyn went to where Bobby and his volunteers were stacking hay, Bobby was high up on top of the whole stack. She told him and the volunteers she had two things to share. First, some guy named Bob in Aztec called to say he wanted to help with the cabins. The confirming surprise was a donor's check for $5,000 that had arrived just that morning. The donation was specifically for their cabin project. Bobby, they later laughingly recalled, did some sort of a gleeful hand-waving jig of celebration on top of the hay bales.

Soon after I arrived, Carolyn also revealed she'd been praying for another "Bobby." She had prayerfully intended the Lord should send them a guy who worked as hard as her husband. Her prayers were answered, and with someone who had the name Bob too.

Yes, I spent those two weeks, and the rest of the summer and early fall, at Tender Lives Ranch, helping in any way I could. Mary later came up from Aztec to work directly with the young girls, and along with Carolyn, later in the season baked tons of peach desserts—luscious pies, cobblers, and more.

Now, here's the more mysterious and interesting part. I didn't help with any of the cabin construction. Bobby Clement had a different idea. You see, he's an old raised-in-the-back-country-of-Oklahoma horse ranch kind of guy who doesn't let just anyone work with his horses. Tender Lives Ranch had seventeen horses. Only a couple of days after I arrived, Bobby told me he and the other volunteers would take care of building the cabins. His time, he explained, would be freed up for those projects if I would take care of the livestock.

That was a curious request, because after working with him for only a little while I knew of his proprietary interest in those horses. "You have a way with 'em," he assured me when I expressed doubt. I finally shrugged and offered that I just did what needed to be done and the horses seemed to cooperate. He said, "In Oklahoma, we call that a gift."

So my summer was spent mostly with two or three mares and their new babies, five geldings, and a half-dozen or so other horses, including a huge former racehorse now out to stud named Blackie. As the apparent "head wrangler" for the summer, I fed and watered and talked to 'em. I bathed 'em and talked some more. I brushed 'em and cleaned their hooves, mucked out their stalls and paddocks, and all the while, I talked to 'em. I helped Bobby and the vet when a couple of those foal babies arrived in the middle of the night. After birthing, the mares need to be walked, so I did that too and talked to 'em. And when the mares were in heat, I even assisted with the studding procedures, if you know what I mean. And, yes, I talked to the mares then to help them stay as calm as possible.

I loved getting up on those brisk mountain mornings when the sun peeked over the tops of the Unaweep Canyon walls, putting on my work boots on the front porch of the ranch house, and then making the gravel-crunching walk between the pine trees to my first stop, the mare barn. The air was always crisp. The only background sounds I recall were from birds and an occasional neigh from beyond my sight. As I made the right turn on the driveway going away from the ranch house, I could always count on seeing at least two horsey heads looking expectantly my way: a little one and a big one. Mamas and babies knew who was coming to give them breakfast, and they were always polite and appreciative as I served them.

The geldings were a little different. In fact, they were usually a rowdy bunch. With them, I had to be stronger and more forceful, unquestionably letting them know who was boss. The alpha in this herd was me. If they wanted to eat, they'd have to do it my way and in my timing. I talked to them, too, but just a little louder.

The summer passed quickly. Although I did some riding to help Bobby train a few of the horses for trail work for the fall elk hunting parties and also a little trail riding with the campers, my time was mostly invested with those seventeen horses and the projects I created around the ranch. I mended fences and talked to horses. I repaired a barn roof and jabbered with horses. I built a ramp for training the skittish ones to get into and out of a trailer, and I talked to them while doing it. The labor, outdoors, surrounded by pine trees and canyon walls, was refreshing no matter how hard I sweat or how dirty I got.

Bobby tended to be a nonstop, sunup-to-sunset kind of worker, so while talking to curious horses watching over paddock fences, I built a couple of "sit-a-spell" benches, one next to the mare barn, the other one close to the geldings. I urged Bobby to take a break once in a while to appreciate the beauty of the canyon and their ranch . . . and the horses. There were lots of other chores, the kind that ranchers and farmers know do not end. There were also hikes and campfires with guitar-and-singing sessions, and Sunday services in a beautiful log cabin church Bobby pastored a ways north of the ranch.

Mary and I were blessed in many ways by the people we shared life with during our time at Tender Lives Ranch. But my time was blessed most of all working with those seventeen horses. Curiously, I haven't had an opportunity to work with any since that time. However, I guess I heard God right after all back there in Aztec, New Mexico. I really was supposed to work on a horse ranch in Colorado.

Why Do the Amish Keep Their Horse and Buggies?

In the 1920s, as the automobile was emerging on the American landscape, the Old Order Amish had a presentiment: the automobile would fracture families and tight-knit communities. Not all Amish agreed. At the time, car ownership versus horse-drawn transportation became the cause for several church divisions. The Old Order Amish wouldn't budge. Turning their backs on the car, they retained their horse culture.

Today, the horse is more than a symbol for the Old Order Amish. It's a metaphor that represents the values and ideals they hold dear. In a striking show of nonconformity, the horse separates the Amish from the modern, hectic world. It restricts mobility, preserves a link to nature, enhances community, limits the size of tillable farm acreage, anchors the people to their past. Best of all, the Amish insist—and, frankly, it's hard to argue—a horse slows down the pace of life.

—Suzanne Woods Fisher

They Rode to Victory

Mary C. Busha

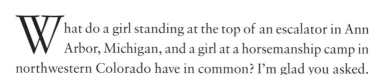

W hat do a girl standing at the top of an escalator in Ann Arbor, Michigan, and a girl at a horsemanship camp in northwestern Colorado have in common? I'm glad you asked.

First let me tell you about the young girl on the escalator. One Christmas season I worked retail at Macy's in Ann Arbor, Michigan. My job was on the second floor in children's wear. On a Sunday afternoon I heard a commotion at the top of the escalator just outside our department. I walked over to see what was going on, and there was a young girl, about ten, an older woman I guessed to be her mom, and a couple of other people who appeared to be curious bystanders.

"May I help you?" I asked the one I thought to be the mom.

"She's afraid to go down the escalator," she responded. By the expression on the young girl's face, that's exactly what it looked like, so I motioned to the elevator not ten feet away.

"She needs to go down the escalator," came next from the mom, and then I realized we had a lesson going on. I stepped back.

No amount of coaxing could get that little girl to step onto that escalator and take the ride down. Mama's words didn't help. Nor did the words of one of the bystanders who began quoting Scripture: "God hath not given us the spirit of fear; but of power, and of love, and of a sound mind."[6] The bystander then told the girl to repeat those words and to take the first step. All the young girl could do, however, was look at her mama and then down to the first floor with fear so thick you could cut it if that were possible.

All of a sudden, without even realizing what I was doing, I spoke to the girl and said, "I can do everything through Christ, who gives me strength."[7]

The girl took one look at me, and then, miracle of miracles, she stepped onto that escalator and rode down. Once she got to the bottom, she turned around and looked back up to those of us who cheered her on. She smiled so big I thought I could see the department store lights reflect brightly in her beautiful teeth.

Little did I know that very experience would speak to a little girl around the same age just six months later at Tender Lives Ranch in Colorado's beautiful Unaweep Canyon.

My husband, Bob, and I had accepted an invitation to work at the ranch the next summer. Bob tended to the horses on this twenty-acre ranch, and I met every morning with the ten girls who had come to take part in the weeklong program designed to teach them the ins and outs of horsemanship and to raise their level of confidence and self-awareness. Some of the girls had experience; most did not. But by the end of the week, they would know how to ride, groom, muck out the stalls, and truly have an appreciation for these majestic four-footed creatures.

My job was to encourage and inspire the girls with morning devotions. I noticed one girl in particular, Missy, was quite fearful. She dressed the part and talked the talk, but when it came time to actually get on a horse, she was scared stiff. She did well in all the lessons except riding, because once in the saddle, all she wanted to do was get back down. And I can't say I blamed her. That horse stood head and shoulders above this little girl. I'm not sure I could have mustered the courage to get up there and ride.

One morning I strayed from my script and told the story about the girl at the top of the escalator. I watched the girls, especially Missy, to see if perhaps my words struck a chord. I still saw fear in her eyes. And my heart broke for her. She so wanted her parents to be proud of her when they came for the last day of camp. But now we weren't even sure if she was going to be able to ride.

With each passing day, Missy got a little further along in her riding lessons. On day five, family members and friends arrived, and so did the time for gymkhana, when the girls would demonstrate what they had learned, maneuvering their horses in and around the barrels placed for that purpose.

One by one the girls rode past the admiring crowd. And then it was Missy's turn. Oh, how I wanted to grab her up in my arms and protect her. But those running the program knew better than I did, and they helped her up onto her horse. I sat on the edge of my seat as I watched Missy slowly but surely maneuver her steed with a confidence I had not seen in her before that day. She rode around each barrel—cautiously, yes, but with grace. When she reached the finish line, she looked over at us all with a huge smile of accomplishment. I imagined there was relief there too.

We all jumped to our feet and cheered. Everyone was on the one hand relieved and on the other elated for this little girl's accomplishment in just a few short days.

Once Missy, the last of the riders, dismounted, the ceremonies began. Each of the girls walked by the stands to receive our congratulations and then to the camp leaders to receive their certificates of graduation. Photos were taken, hugs were given, and then Missy found me in the crowd. She said, "I did it, Miss Mary," to which I replied, "I know, Missy, and we're all so proud of you."

"I said those words, Miss Mary. When I got up on my horse, I said, 'I can do everything through Christ, who gives me strength.'"

I had no words at that point, but I did have a few tears.

And then I realized that the little girl in Ann Arbor and the little girl in Colorado had one more thing in common. They both conquered their respective fears with the help of God, and they rode on to victory. One rode an escalator; the other rode a horse.

The Horse Farm

Donna Acton

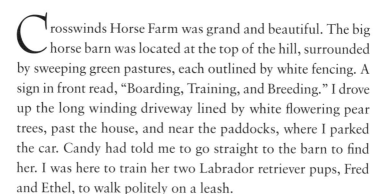

Crosswinds Horse Farm was grand and beautiful. The big horse barn was located at the top of the hill, surrounded by sweeping green pastures, each outlined by white fencing. A sign in front read, "Boarding, Training, and Breeding." I drove up the long winding driveway lined by white flowering pear trees, past the house, and near the paddocks, where I parked the car. Candy had told me to go straight to the barn to find her. I was here to train her two Labrador retriever pups, Fred and Ethel, to walk politely on a leash.

I found Candy pushing open one of the huge barn doors on its sliding track. She waved to me. "Come on in—I just have to finish putting the last few horses out in the pasture."

I walked out of the bright summer sunlight and into the cool, quiet alley of the barn. I breathed in the rich scent of fresh-cut timothy hay. A big bay was on the cross ties in the aisle of the

110

barn that was lined with wooden horse stalls, most of them open and empty.

"I have to clean his feet first," Candy said, holding up a hoof pick. "It'll take just a minute." She turned to the horse, patted his shoulder, and said, "You're a real good boy, aren't you, Junior?" She sidled up to Junior's shoulder and lifted his hoof to the top of her thigh. With a few expert strokes with the hoof pick, she cleaned the first hoof and was done with the fourth in no time. With the same deft motions, Candy snapped on Junior's lead rope and unsnapped both cross ties.

"I like to check everyone's feet once a day," she said as she passed me with the big gelding. I watched as she opened a pasture gate, swung Junior around to face her, and then released him. He paused, ducked his head ever so slightly before pivoting on his hind legs, swinging his head high. Then he raced up the grassy slope at top speed. Candy stood with her hands on her hips, smiling.

Returning to the barn she passed me at a brisk pace. "I just have one more horse to move." I sat on a tack box as she slid open the big door at the other end of the barn. Beyond the door I could see a cavernous indoor riding arena with a large chestnut horse pawing the ground.

"Stand back," Candy said. "This guy is a Thoroughbred, and he's got a lot of energy." With a swift, practiced motion, Candy opened the gate, walked in, and snapped the lead rope to his halter. "Capone," she said with authority, giving the lead rope a small tug. "Settle down."

Capone pranced out of the arena, head high, neck arched, and fiery. I could see from my spot on the tack box that Capone was starting to inch into Candy's space. After a few more steps he was truly crowding her against the wall of one of the stalls.

Candy's correction with her voice and her tug on the lead rope were quick and solid. Capone backed off and quieted down for the rest of his walk to the pasture.

Watching this interaction between Capone and Candy, I figured I should have no problem with Candy and her two dogs. She already knew how to assume the attitude of commanding respect from the horse. I would simply have to translate that into working with her dogs and their leashes.

I'm very good at communicating with dogs. I have worked with them for many years. I know what they are saying to me and what they are thinking, and I am able to tell them what I want them to do. Although I owned a horse for a couple of years as a teenager, I can only talk to horses when I am on their back, holding the reins. I was never able to communicate with a horse when I was on the ground and still cannot. But Candy knew how to do that.

"Time to meet Fred and Ethel," Candy said, leading me past the stalls. As I followed her, I wondered if I had ever seen such a clean barn. The center aisle of cement had been freshly swept, and not a loose strand of hay or straw could be seen. Each of the open stalls had been cleaned and filled with fresh bedding.

The dogs were in the last stall on the left. Fred was a yellow Labrador and Ethel was black, and they each looked to be about seventy pounds.

"These are the puppies?" I asked. "They're sort of big."

"Well, I still think of them as my babies," Candy said. She slid open the stall door and cooed to them. "You're my big babies, aren't you?"

Fred and Ethel exploded out of the stall like wild balls of energy, running up and down the barn's main aisle. They crashed into the doors, the walls, each other, and finally into

Candy and me. Fred and Ethel were telling me loud and clear they had no respect for my personal space or Candy's. Both dogs ignored Candy's pleadings of "Stay down, honey" and "Please sit."

But Candy laughed. "They have no manners. Aren't they cute?"

I could tell Candy was misjudging their maturity and being too soft. They were literally running over her. When I questioned Candy about the dogs, she told me they slept in the house but accompanied her to the barn whenever she was doing chores, and she claimed they were great around the horses.

"Let me get their leashes," Candy said. "I'll show you what I'm having trouble with."

She snapped leashes on both dogs, and we left the barn. Both Fred and Ethel strained forward. With a leash in each hand, Candy leaned back like a water skier. Each step of hers skidded across the long grass as we crossed the hay field. I was practically running, trying to keep up with them. When we reached the hedgerow of trees and rock wall between the hay field and the cornfield, I had to stop her.

"Candy, hold up," I said. "Doesn't that pulling hurt your arms?"

"Yes, just terrible," she said. "Last week they pulled me down, and I twisted my ankle. It swelled up like a football."

We were now two fields away from the farm road they lived on. There was a field of soy beans on my left, and through the hedgerow of oak trees on my right was another cornfield. I felt we were safe from car traffic, and I wanted to observe the dogs' behavior, so I said, "Let them off their leashes."

Candy froze. She looked at me with fear in her eyes, then she looked at Fred and Ethel, who were now both jumping on her.

"Turn them loose," I said.

"I can't turn them loose. They'll go in the road and get hit by a car."

"We're nowhere near the road."

"But you see how strong they are. They'll just run, and I'll never find them again." She truly looked frightened.

I spent some time explaining the behavior of Labradors to Candy. "They'll think they're hunting with us," I said. "Trust me, they will stay with us. That's what they were bred for."

But Candy's fear was palpable. Both dogs continued to jerk her arms to the left and to the right. Then both dogs jumped up on her chest and raked her with their toenails.

"I can't do it," she said.

"Trust me," I said again.

Candy steadied herself and snapped the leashes off the dogs. Fred and Ethel exploded like rockets off a launch pad, running straight ahead through the trees and into the swale.

Candy looked at me with desperation. "See?" she yelled as she started to run after them. "I told you they'd run away."

"Don't chase them! Come with me!" I said, running to the nearest oak tree in the hedgerow. "Get behind me, Candy. We're going to hide from Fred and Ethel."

"How will they find us?"

"They're hunting dogs," I reminded her. "We are forcing them to hunt for us. They're young dogs and not as sure of themselves as you think they are. In a minute or two, they're going to be worried about where you are. Just wait."

Fred and Ethel ran back in a few minutes and stopped in the grassy two-track cut between the fields. Fred started sniffing the ground and Ethel sniffed the air, looking in every direction with darting glances. They both looked mystified.

I could tell they didn't know what to do. I spoke quietly to Candy. "We're going to teach them to come when called right now."

I whistled for the dogs and called both of their names. I heard and felt them thundering toward us. The moment they saw us, Fred and Ethel's faces turned from confusion to joy and relief. So did Candy's.

"You're right," Candy said. "They came to look for us."

"Of course they did. They're Labradors. What they learned today was that they have to stay close and keep an eye on you because you could disappear at the drop of a hat."

As I talked, both dogs jumped up on Candy and raked her with their toenails again. "Tell them *Off*," I said.

Candy continued petting and cooing to them. "But they're such good dogs. They didn't run away. They came back."

We walked for an hour with the dogs running off leash until they were finally tuckered out. We put them back on leash, and they walked quietly back to the barn. I wondered how I was going to turn Candy into the strong leader I needed her to be with her dogs. Inside the barn, however, I saw Candy flip immediately from indulgent dog owner to commanding horsewoman.

We heard pounding hoof strikes against the wall of a stall half way down. "I have to move this Welsh pony," Candy said. She grabbed a lead rope, slid open the stall door, and Ginger exploded out, kicking and bucking. Candy kept a tight grip on the lead rope and kept Ginger's head close to her shoulder. "Settle, Ginger," she said with a smart tug to the halter. "Settle." As they walked out the front door to a paddock, Ginger did indeed settle down.

"There," I said. "That's the attitude I need from you when training Fred and Ethel."

"Dogs are different," Candy said. "I have to be this strong with horses. They can kill you. You can never give them an inch. Especially a firebrand like Ginger."

This is where I spend my time trying to draw from the owner's experience—whether the person is a schoolteacher or a prison guard or the owner of a horse farm—to translate what they already know into working and training their dogs. Candy could communicate with horses, understand what they were saying, and get them to comply with what she wanted.

Now I had to translate the use of the halter to a dog collar and the use of the lead rope to a leash until Candy could view them as the same. She would be able communicate what she wanted to the dogs with those tools just as she communicated with her horses. I reminded Candy what she well knew—while dogs aren't as big and dangerous as horses, they could injure her if out of control.

It worked. The dog training went well. It went so well that Fred and Ethel became lovely dogs to move through the fields off leash and on. When Candy stood, hands on her hips, and whistled for them, they ran to her. They were no longer unsafe to their owner, because she was in control.

Just like with her horses.

The Horse Who Taught Me to Take a Second Look

Nicole M. Miller

My mother and I waited at the Chevron station along Interstate 5, eyes peeled for a truck and horse trailer exiting the highway.

It was our last chance to say good-bye.

Eight months earlier, when this straggly, four-year-old, chestnut Thoroughbred gelding arrived at my house, I was annoyed. I had grown out of my Arabian mare and wanted something more flashy for the 4-H show ring.

A racetrack reject was not what I'd wanted.

He'd been abandoned. He needed a home. Our family friend, who was a trainer at Emerald Downs track in Washington, had heard about this starved, neglected horse. He knew we'd provide a good home.

Southern Buddar was too clumsy to be of any use on the racetrack. His knees were as knobby as coconuts and his hooves as wide as platters. His withers arched high on his back, emphasized by the lack of fat and protruding ribs. He had a long face, Roman nose, and tiny eyes. I couldn't show this gelding. I couldn't even ride him—he was barely broken.

Full of fifteen-year-old pride and wisdom, I made it clear that this was my mom's horse, not mine. I only cared about my own riding career. I couldn't win any ribbons with an ugly horse. And this oafish Thoroughbred joining the family meant that finding my next show horse would be delayed.

Great.

When he arrived he was nervous, shaking, and thin. So thin. My mother kept him on a steady diet of hay, petting, and carrots. I kept my distance.

During the first few months of "Bud's" residency, my mare exhibited her dominance and picked on him incessantly. The 14.2-hand Arabian had the 17-hand Thoroughbred running for cover. In our greenness as horse owners, we didn't separate them quickly enough, thinking they'd work out their differences.

They did, in a way.

One night, a thunderous bang echoed from inside the large, open stall they shared, and we found Buddar with his back hoof severed and nearly cut off.

Since our barn and pasture were thick with mud and the stalls were open for turnout 24/7, we took Buddar to a nearby stable for recovery.

The hoof was wrapped, cleaned, rewrapped, and it needed to be treated daily. I helped my mom even though I disliked this horse. Our "free" horse was far from free. He required a lot of time and money, which detracted from the showing I wanted to do.

One of the first times I changed the bandages myself, the irritated gelding jerked his foot free and kicked out enough to hit my thigh and give me an eggplant-size-and-color bruise. I grumbled but finished wrapping and treating the wound. *Ungrateful.*

As the days turned into weeks, changing the bandages became a routine task, and Bud accepted it without protest. As he recovered from the pain, built up his body mass, and settled into life at the stables, his personality rose to the surface, and I came to expect soft nuzzles and perked ears. I even took him carrots regularly.

I started working at the stables and was around Bud more and more. As we neared the end of his recovery, he nickered whenever he saw me (or the carrots in my hand). When he was sound once more, my mom decided Bud was too much horse for her, and we needed to sell him. We knew he'd be a great project for another family to take on. And he was healthy, fit, and in one piece. Finally.

We left him at the stables while we placed an ad so potential buyers could ride him in a covered arena. One evening we received a frantic call from the barn owner—Bud had eaten some wet hay and was in the throes of colic. My mom and I raced to the barn. We pushed, shoved, and tugged that horse to his feet and kept him slogging along to keep him from surrendering to the stomachache.

We alternated walking him. Bud held his head steady next to mine, his small, black eyes pleading and sorrowful. His thick Roman nose tapered into a small muzzle that brushed my hands every so often.

In those long hours, I realized I didn't hate this horse. I didn't hate him at all.

I didn't want him to die.

It was nearly dawn by the time Bud pulled through his colic and returned to his bumbling, friendly self. He was in the clear. I went back to "hating" him, but it was a farce. I loved the racetrack reject.

We found a young woman interested in Bud as an eventing prospect. They got along with him splendidly. His foot had healed, and it was time for him to move on. It was time for me to get back to what I wanted to do. I had another horse by this time, and my showing career kept me focused.

"Give him lots of carrots," I requested as we signed the papers and Bud was loaded into the trailer.

But when Buddar and his new family pulled away, I cried.

Months later Bud's new family called us. He'd been diagnosed with a neurological disease, and they planned to put him down.

My mom sprang into action. She called the Oregon State University Veterinary School and discovered they would take the gelding to run experimental treatments on this untreatable disease. They assured us he would be spoiled with carrots until the very end.

We convinced the new owners to take the horse from Washington State to Corvallis, Oregon. We asked if we could meet them along the way to say our good-byes.

Sitting in the car, waiting for the truck and trailer to appear, I desperately clung to the emotions I had when we first got Buddar. He was ugly. He was clumsy. He wasn't what I wanted.

But he'd been the horse I needed. He taught me that affection and connection don't always come right away. Sometimes there's a diamond underneath the scruffy brown fur and dinner-plate hooves.

The truck and trailer parked next to us in the gas station. My mom made small talk with the owners. I walked straight to the trailer and lowered the window. Buddar's head, the length of my torso, jutted out, and he glanced around nervously.

My tears fell swiftly as I petted his nose. He sniffed my hand and nickered softly. My mom petted him, shed her tears, spoke to the owners again, and thanked them

I couldn't say anything other than, "Good-bye, Bud."

We closed the trailer window. The diesel truck rumbled out of the parking lot and back onto the interstate, headed for Bud's last home.

I cried all the way home, my excuses for hating him now invalid.

He was ugly. But those little eyes and big head were quirky, almost cartoon-like.

He was clumsy. But he taught me to move my feet a bit faster so as not to be stepped on.

He wasn't what I wanted. But I'd had no idea what I'd wanted.

I still don't. But I learned to look beyond that first glance. I never know when another free racetrack reject might bumble into my life. So I always look twice.

A few weeks later we called the veterinary program and asked how Bud was doing. They said he was getting fat on carrots because everyone loved him so much and wouldn't stop giving him the treat.

Southern Buddar couldn't have ended up in a better place.

Determined Little Giant

Catherine Ulrich Brakefield

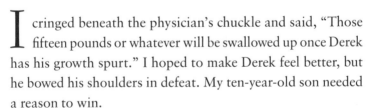

I cringed beneath the physician's chuckle and said, "Those fifteen pounds or whatever will be swallowed up once Derek has his growth spurt." I hoped to make Derek feel better, but he bowed his shoulders in defeat. My ten-year-old son needed a reason to win.

Derek hated leaving his best friend behind when he switched schools at the end of fourth grade. His new school was larger, and the fifth grade boys had full authority on the playground. Derek came home with bruises he always had excuses for. What could I do to boost his morale?

A well-known horse breeder in Indiana needed to downsize his herd. We drove out to look at a handsome five-year-old black Arabian gelding, 14.2 hands tall. Though his height was small for a horse, it was perfect for Derek.

With Eclipse, Derek could enter 4-H and the Arabian horse shows. Could Eclipse be the morale booster Derek needed, or would this prove another disappointment for my son?

My husband and I trailered Eclipse to our Michigan home. Derek wanted to ride him immediately. The trainer's undesired words popped into my mind. "I always lunge him for at least fifteen minutes before riding him. I suggest you do the same."

I told my son I wanted to ride him first. Eclipse walked the trail calmly and I relaxed, but the trainer's words continued to haunt me, remembering what he had said to me. "You don't look big on him." Why had he said that when he knew I was purchasing Eclipse for my son?

I gave Eclipse the canter cue. He lowered his head between his front legs, rolled his back like a beach ball, and let me have it. I thought I was on a bucking bronco. I think I must have been jolted a good three inches above the saddle! There was no way my young son could handle him. I was ready to pack up Eclipse and send him back to Indiana.

Derek, however, was sympathetic toward Eclipse. "Mom, give him a chance." Derek rubbed Eclipse's head. "He could be scared that no one will like him, and he's trying not to show it."

"Is that what happens to you at this new school?"

Derek shrugged. "I know he's not a quitter. Eclipse thinks he's got to be tough so people can't see he's scared."

Derek had opened up about his school chums. What more would my son's relationship with Eclipse reveal?

"Mom, why don't we take him with us to Little Manistee? You could ride Eclipse and I could ride Lea."

This was our first time to go on a competitive distance ride. Friday after work my husband, our daughter Kim, Derek, and I left for Michigan's northern wilderness located near Lake

Michigan. We signed in and chose the twenty-five-mile endurance ride, which we had to complete in four hours. To win in our respective weight and age divisions, our horses had to pass four veterinarian checkpoints. Our other horses had ridden cross-country numerous times. But could Eclipse do this? I wasn't sure.

The weather forecast for this mid-June Saturday morning was a sizzling eighty-five degrees. We vet-checked in, and after about an hour and half of riding, Eclipse showed signs of being tired. I glanced down at the two inches of sand, then up at the steep hill looming like Mt. Everest ahead. *He's not going to make it.*

After the hill, I pulled him up. I decided to drop out of the race, follow the red flags in a walk, and allow my family to compete. When Eclipse saw his group leaving him, I could tell he thought, *No way!*

It was just as Derek had thought. On the outside Eclipse was small, but not on the inside. He was a little giant inside and no quitter. He and my son had a lot in common. Eclipse got his second wind, and we were off. We passed the halfway marker and rested our horses for the mandatory twenty minutes before completing the final leg of the race. Eclipse's vital signs were well below the requirements.

The competition had started out with over one hundred horses. Riders were eliminated because the vital signs of their horses disqualified them. I counted about fifty horses left. The final miles sped by.

The numbers were tallied, and Derek won youth division. His face beamed his joy. Kim won junior division; I won fifth in lightweight and Edward fourth in heavyweight. But the best reward I received that day was that Eclipse never bucked again.

Derek rode him in his first 4-H show the next weekend. Though they did not place, Derek was smiling from ear to ear.

He and Eclipse worked on their patterns and gaits during the week. I stopped worrying about Derek getting hurt on Eclipse. He and this little giant of a horse had developed a special bond. Eclipse seemed to know what Derek wanted before he asked. It felt like Eclipse had picked Derek to befriend and not the other way around.

Derek took Eclipse to the hunt meets and rode him cross-country. The two had the best time running up and down the hills. I could see a change in Derek's personality. He smiled more, he stood straighter, and his laugh grew more frequent and confident each day. He'd found the friend who could boost his self-image.

The 4-H events were a challenge. Derek's hunt classes had well over fifteen participants, and he was usually the youngest rider. We'd drive up, and as soon as Derek saw the trophy for first place, he'd say, "That's mine and Eclipse's." The two of them eventually made it to the 4-H State Championships, winning in Hunt Seat Pleasure.

From small open horse shows to Kentucky Horse Park and Canadian Breeders Championship, Derek and Eclipse were unbeatable—at least in Derek's eyes. He had learned winning was a state of mind. He competed for the enjoyment of sharing the unique camaraderie of this sport that blended horse and rider into an inseparable unit.

Come September, Derek entered school and sports. The boys continued to bully him, but he'd laugh them off. He had a thousand-pound friend, and he didn't need these puny guys.

As Derek's independence grew, so did his sense of responsibility. He took on more of the chores around the stable. Horses needed to be fed, groomed, and ridden. Bringing in fifty-pound hay bales in the summer and mucking out stalls throughout the months, Derek grew over a foot taller. He ate enough food for two and still stayed muscular and lean. By the time Derek entered junior high, he had grown and matured, most importantly from inside out. From his master-servant responsibilities providing for Eclipse, Derek realized he hadn't lost his real best friend. God had been waiting for Derek to notice him, providing Eclipse to boost his morale.

Derek joined the equestrian team in the ninth grade. His team consisted of thirteen riders, and he was the only male. He entered Eclipse in everything from hunt, showmanship, and patterns to keyhole and flags and barrels. Eclipse remained the determined little giant. Derek's confidence grew.

But the day came when Derek had to face the truth. He was six foot one. He had outgrown Eclipse. My husband and I told Derek he could keep him, but Derek knew he needed to say good-bye to his loyal friend.

Derek stroked Eclipse's neck as I had seen him do countless times before. He sniffed. "That wouldn't be fair to Eclipse. He doesn't want to be just a pasture horse."

Though we never advertised, word got around. The little giant Eclipse had made a reputation for himself.

The day Derek took Eclipse out for their last ride, I had tears in my eyes. Derek handed his reins over to the little girl, whose grin was almost as big as she was. I heard Eclipse took that little girl all the way to the Arabian Nationals.

Derek went on to become a public school fifth grade teacher. The Golden Rule, "And just as you want men to do to you, you also do to them likewise," became one of his class fundamentals.[8] And a little statue of a black horse rests on his desk to remind him of a friend who gave him a reason to win.

Go, Horse, Go!

Horsepower is a commonly used unit for measuring the rate at which work is done. Use of the term started in the early nineteenth century, invented by James Watt, the same Mr. Watt whose name we use when speaking of lightbulbs. Watt wanted to measure the amount of power coal mining horses had when pulling up coal. He determined that one horse could pull up thirty-three pounds of coal at a rate of a thousand feet per minute—and 33,000 "foot pounds" per minute equaled one unit of horsepower. The use of the word *horsepower* found its way into all kinds of power measurements, and there's much more to understand about how horsepower is translated. But the astounding thing is that this rate measurement originally based on the power of horses so long ago is still used today—even sometimes for vacuum sweepers.

The Lady and the Scamp

Wanda Dyson

My husband, Jim, owned a horse or two when he was in his teens, but eventually he moved to the suburbs and had to give them up. Now, some twenty years later, he wanted to give up the house in the suburbs and move to the country, find a little farm, and buy another horse or two. It took us over a year of looking before he finally settled on a place nestled in the valley below Camp David. It was a pretty two-story Colonial on just over five acres, with a barn, tack room, paddock, and pasture.

Not long after we moved in, we heard about a local horse auction that took place every two weeks. It was a whole new world to me—one of leather and bits and bridles and saddles. I soon learned that not all saddles are comfortable and not all bits are the same. Try putting the wrong bit on a horse and you could have a battle on your hands. There was one palomino whose owner was going to sell him to the meat man because every time they put the hackamore on him, he'd rear up. Well, a hackamore cuts off their air, so they can't breathe. This horse wasn't about to have any of that. Once someone was smart enough to put a snaffle bit in his mouth, he turned into one of the best cow horses in the county.

I was fascinated. Hooked. And I couldn't learn enough, fast enough.

It was a cold February night, and in spite of the snow, we were at the auction as always. As the snow piled up, the crowd thinned out. We were thinking of leaving when Jim saw a horse trailer pull in and start unloading horses. Jim said he wanted to get a closer look and wandered back where they were checking the horses in.

Jim had stated emphatically that we would not be buying our first horse until spring, and while I was disappointed, the auctions were giving me enough of a horse fix to keep me happy. So nothing could have surprised me more than when Jim sat down in the bleachers and asked me to go get a bidding card. When I asked him why, he said he might need it. And sure enough, a little bit later, he started to bid on a little Appaloosa mare that had just come in. Nearly everyone was gone, so Jim didn't have many bidders to compete with.

He won final bid at $600. Unheard of for a registered trail horse. Her name? Springtime Lady.

When I asked him why he bought her, he replied, "I like the way she looks. Something tells me she's smarter than I am."

Those words would come back to haunt me many times over the fifteen years we owned that little mare. She was smart enough to know when I merely draped her lead rope and had not tied it securely; she'd just trot away. Smart enough to know when the gates were locked and when the chains were just wrapped a couple of times. Smart enough to pretend to limp so I'd get down to check her hooves, then snap the reins from my hand and run home, leaving me to walk home. And smart enough to know how to work the latch of the feed room with her lips and get to the grain.

A man came to our farm one day, and after seeing Lady out in the field, offered us $2,000 for her. We refused but asked why he'd offer so much for a $600 horse. He asked if I had her papers and if I'd checked out her pedigree. He told us she was the spitting image of a horse named Bright Eyes Brother, a foundation horse for the Appaloosa breed. I started doing some research. Sure enough, she was a direct descendant of Bright Eyes himself. And I found out the man who owned Bright Eyes was still alive. I called him and told him I had a great-granddaughter of Bright Eyes, and the first thing he said was, "Smartest horse you've ever seen, isn't she?"

The second horse we bought was a quarter horse named Scooter, but we tended to call him Scamp because of his mischievous ways. He and Lady were inseparable. She ruled the roost, but you could tell she adored Scamp.

We had those two horses—and a few more—when a friend came over and wanted to take his girlfriend on a horseback ride. I gave them Lady and Scamp because I trusted those two to be out there on the road with people who were, at best, moderate riders.

I was folding laundry about an hour later when I heard the front door crash open and what sounded like metal banging on my hardwood floors.

I ran out and was met in the hallway by none other than Lady herself, prancing along the floors, clearly agitated. I backed her out of the house, trying to figure out how she managed to open the front door, but she wouldn't let me take her back down to the barn. She continued to yank and pull and whinny, trying to go back down the driveway.

I finally climbed up on her and let her take me to wherever it was she wanted to go so desperately. About a mile down the road, I saw what had upset her. Scamp was standing on the side of the road, head down, blood covering one side of him, and the two riders were standing there like they didn't have a clue what to do.

They told me they had been running the horses down the gravel road when Scamp lost his footing and went down, sliding across the gravel on his side. When the girl dismounted Lady to help her boyfriend, Lady bolted for home.

Scamp could walk, and we all headed back to the house. As soon as we got home, Lady headed down to the barn and waited for me to come unsaddle and brush her. But she wasn't in any hurry. She knew I had to take care of Scamp first.

I called the vet, and we were lucky; Scamp suffered little more than scrapes and minor cuts, but it was still enough for Lady to worry. For about a week she let him eat out of her food bowl and watched him like a mother hen for any sign of further injury. Once she knew he was fine, she went back to pushing him around and guarding her food from him.

As the herd grew, so did Lady's bossiness. In fact, she became quite the tattletale. If a horse found a way through the fence and left the pasture, she'd run to the gate and raise enough of a ruckus to draw Jim or me down to find out what was going on. If one of the horses got hurt, she'd let us know. And when we moved to a farm with 125 acres, she made sure all the horses stayed together, lest any get hurt or escape without her knowledge.

When Scamp died, Lady became a loner, stand-offish with the herd for nearly a year. But that changed when Kris came to us. He was a rescue horse, a spotted Appaloosa who had been abandoned and, by the time he'd been found, was nearly dead from starvation. Within two days Lady had taken Kris as her companion, watching out for him until he regained his health and weight. Within a few weeks we found out just what a rascal Kris was. You could not wear a hat out there in the field. He'd sneak up on you, acting all innocent, and then when you least expected it, would snatch your hat off your head and run away with it.

Lady forever remained Jim's horse, and their love for each other was nonnegotiable. She'd permit someone else to ride her, but you could tell she had an attitude about it. And when Jim died, she moped around the fence line for weeks, watching for him.

Without Jim, I gave up the farm and the horses. One by one they were sold. But Lady would have none of it, acting up for anyone who came to see her. Just a week before the movers came, a man stopped by to check out the two paints—mother and foal. He kept looking at Lady, and Lady kept getting closer and closer until finally she rubbed her head on his arm to get him to pet her.

Lady had chosen her new owner. Now it was up to him to figure it out.

When he made me an offer for the two paints, he asked how much I wanted for Lady.

I told him. Then I added, "Just in case you wondered, she's probably smarter than you are, and you'd be wise not to ever underestimate her. She will have you trained in no time."

The man laughed. "A real princess, eh?"

"No," I replied. "A lady with a soft spot for scamps."

Making the Rounds with Blackie

Susy Flory

When Blackie walks in the door of the hospice center to visit sick children, he generates a ripple of excitement wherever he goes. The kids love to pet him and groom his silky black hair. His eyes are alive and seem to be saying, "Let's do this." His ears point forward, and while he is full of life and energy, he is also quiet and gentle. A wise man once said gentleness is "strength under control." That's Blackie.

Most therapy animals are dogs. Dogs have been partnering with humans for thousands of years to serve in a variety of roles and are quick to establish a strong, therapeutic human-animal bond. But Blackie is not a dog; he's a horse. A miniature horse with a very big job. While most children have either owned a dog or been around dogs, most children do not get the opportunity to be around horses. So it's a special moment when

Blackie clip-clops down the hallway, stops at a sick child's door in the hospice facility, pokes his head in, and enters. It must seem almost too good to be true for a family that has heard too much bad news.

"Blackie is our superstar," said Melanie Buerke of SonRise Equestrian Foundation, a nonprofit organization that creates loving connections between horses and children living with social, emotional, or physical challenges. SonRise puts children on specially trained horses with close supervision for an individualized program of instruction. By learning how to handle and ride horses, children develop confidence, integrity, and a sense of responsibility, along with working on physical, emotional, and cognitive skills. SonRise has both full-size and miniature horses. Blackie is one of six "minis," but he is special.

"Blackie knows what to do and how to approach the kids," said Melanie. "Blackie has a thoughtfulness. His eyes are just expressive, present, *there*. You can look at Blackie and ask him for something. He'll think about it, then do it."

Good therapy animals need to like people, be controllable and teachable, and have good manners and a stable personality. They also need to be able to calmly accept new or unusual sights, sounds, smells, and situations. Blackie fulfills every requirement, plus he passionately loves children.

Melanie never planned on working with miniatures. But right after SonRise got started, she and some of her volunteers were dreaming out loud about how to spread the word about the services they offered the community. "Wouldn't it be great if we had a miniature horse?" someone brainstormed. "We could take it around to festivals and parades. Can you imagine how much attention it would get?" Everyone agreed. But they had no idea where to go or how to find one.

Then Melanie received an unusual phone call. "I heard about who you are and what you are doing," a woman said. "I have a miniature horse named Blackie. He's been a show horse, performed in parades, pulls a cart, and has lots of training. And he *loves* kids. I'm getting married and moving to Switzerland, and I can't take him with me. I want to meet you guys and see if this is a place for Blackie to go."

The woman came out to the ranch located in the golden grassy foothills across the bay from San Francisco. Melanie showed her around the immaculate barns and introduced her to the foundation's gentle, well-mannered, and intelligent horses. She met some of the volunteers and heard more about the vision—to help hurting children thrive simply by receiving unconditional love from a concerned mentor and a special horse, at no cost to their caregivers. Although she had spent many years training Blackie, she knew her little horse would have a very important new job at SonRise.

So Blackie moved in, and everyone fell in love with him. None of the SonRise women had ever worked with a mini before. They discovered Blackie has the same characteristics as a full-size horse, just in a smaller package. Blackie is about the size of a large Rottweiler or German Shepherd, with a shiny black coat and a fluffy black mane and tail. He's surprisingly strong and can pull a cart with two people in it. He can also be ridden by children who might be afraid of riding and handling a larger horse.

As Melanie began to get to know Blackie and to watch him in action at community events, she was impressed with his calm, soothing personality. Yet he wasn't lazy or passive; his active little mind was obvious by the way he watched whatever was going on, ears up and forward. He had plenty of energy and was always quick to learn and to perform, but it was carefully controlled energy harnessed for whatever the situation required.

Then Melanie got another unexpected call. One of the Son-Rise volunteers worked at a local respite care and end-of-life facility for children. She had an idea. Would Melanie bring Blackie over to visit the sick children at the hospice? Melanie wasn't sure how Blackie would react to being indoors, especially in a medical facility. Would the unfamiliar environment bother him? Would he be able to tolerate the beeps and buzzes of the medical monitors and the smells from disinfectants and medications?

There was only one way to tell. Melanie collected a couple of volunteers to help load Blackie in the horse trailer for the short ride to the hospice. When they arrived, he surprised everyone by walking right in like he owned the place. Melanie started with short visits to the facility, gradually acquainting Blackie with his new job. She watched for signs of nervousness or stress and always took him home before he became really uncomfortable.

Melanie decided to take Blackie through the certification process for Pet Partners therapy program. "It was incredible," said Melanie. "We went through training together and Blackie was dynamite. During the test to see how Blackie might react in unusual situations, they tried to scare him with loud noises—a guy hit him on the hindquarters and yelled, and they shook noisemakers around him. There was some weird stuff going on. But Blackie just stood and looked."

Blackie graduated from the program with flying colors and was certified at the highest level possible. He and Melanie began to visit the children at the hospice regularly. And it wasn't long before Blackie felt right at home. Every month Blackie and Melanie made the rounds. The mini marched into each room and allowed himself to be stroked and brushed and patted, spreading his own fuzzy brand of hope and healing.

"It's almost like magic," Melanie said. "We can go into a room where a child is ill. The mom, dad, and siblings will be there around the edges of the bed, so sad. Sometimes you feel like you can cut the atmosphere with a knife, it's so heavy with grief and pain. But Blackie walks in, clip-clop, and everything changes. It's like he brings light and fresh air into the room. It's a moment no one ever forgets."

Blackie also visited convalescent homes, where seniors loved him. His presence often reminded them of happy childhood memories. For many of them horses were part of daily life growing up, and petting Blackie helped them remember those happy times. He's just as comfortable with an older person as he is with a child.

After Blackie had been making his rounds for a few months, a call came in with an emergency request for a special, unscheduled visit. A little girl named Francine[9] was very ill. Her parents had checked her into the end-of-life facility so she could spend the last part of her life in a comfortable, cheerful place where her family could enjoy time together in a life-affirming, supportive environment.

Francine loved horses, and when Melanie walked into the room, she noticed a fluffy stuffed horse on the dresser. But the room was awash in sadness. The parents were huddled in a corner. Francine's grandmother was in the other corner. In the middle of the room was the bed where Francine lay. She had been going in and out of a comatose state for a while now, and it was almost impossible to rouse her.

In walked Blackie, clip-clop, ears perky and eyes shining, life and love and energy in a compact package of hair and tail and hooves. He looked around and took in the room, then approached the bed. He walked up until his chest gently bumped against the covers on the side of the bed and gently lowered his head onto the bed. His chin and whiskery lips ever so softly nudged the little girl's hand.

The nurse gently shook Francine's arm. "Honey, Blackie's here." No response. Francine slept on.

"Francine, Blackie's here to see you." Francine stirred, then moved her head and slowly opened her eyes. Her parents, who had been waiting in the corner to see what would happen, jumped up. Francine was waking up.

Melanie began to talk softly to the girl, and when she seemed ready, helped her to reach over and touch Blackie's head. His coat radiated warmth and life, and the girl began to stroke him, her hand moving slowly. Her eyes opened wider and her body shifted a bit. Then she smiled, and the room suddenly grew brighter.

It's hard to put into words, but there is something majestic and beautiful and powerful when a horse trusts someone enough to make friends. Like dogs, horses live in community, and when they allow a human into that community there is a special bond.

Everyone in Francine's room felt that bond. Francine's smile grew, and her parents began to take pictures as she sat, propped up by some pillows, and began to slowly brush Blackie with a soft bristle brush Melanie put in her hand. Blackie kept his head still, allowing the girl to groom his mane and forelock. For about fifteen minutes, Francine was happy, lighting up the room with her shining face as she stroked and talked to the little black horse with his head perched on her bed. Then she grew tired, lay back, and began to fade. As her eyes grew heavy and she became drowsy again, Melanie knew it was time to leave. She took Blackie's lead rope and led him quietly out of the room, glancing one last time at Francine and then at her stuffed horse. This was the day Francine made friends with a real live horse.

The next day Melanie heard the news from her friend who worked at the facility. After Melanie and Blackie left, Francine was tired but awake and alert enough to talk to her mom, dad, and grandma. She told them how much she loved them and they spent some precious moments together. It was a bittersweet time. Francine's body was failing, but the visit from Blackie had woken the little girl up, put a smile on her face, and unlocked an outpouring of love and tenderness between the family, allowing them the chance to say good-bye.

That was the last time Francine was ever awake. But some of her very last moments alive were spent with Blackie, her hand on his nose, his warm breath tickling her skin.

Allegro Amabile

Clyde McKaney

I was ten years old, riding my bike around town. In the park at the city's edge, I noticed there was a riding stable. I stopped and watched the horses—some roaming the field, some tied to the fence, some in paddocks in the front. A city boy, I had never been around horses, and right away they fascinated me with their graceful movement and beauty.

For the next couple of weeks, I was a nuisance at the stable because I wanted to be around those horses. There were about sixty of them. I asked my mother to take my younger brother and me to ride. My ride was wonderfully fun, and as we were led around, the owners talked about how to ride. I wound up taking the reins myself and was hooked.

Every day I rode my bike the fifteen city blocks to the stable at the edge of town and hung out there. I spent my allowance riding—it was about four dollars an hour. I chose the same horse every time—a pure white mare named Snowflake. She was my favorite to ride, although I enjoyed watching all the horses run in the pasture. In fact, sometimes I'd be a little naughty and stir things up so they'd take off and I could watch them run. That's when I felt the magic of what they were.

Once the stable people saw I had an affinity for horses and would not be a liability, they let me help out as much as I wanted. I mucked stalls and helped brush horses and clean hooves. I loved being there. I paid special attention to Snowflake—so much so that when I was eleven years old, the stable owner said to me, "You really do like her, don't you?" He offered to sell her to me for $85.

The surprise on my parents' faces was priceless when I went home—to our house in town—and asked them to buy me a horse. Somehow I talked them into it. My parents also paid Snowflake's board for a few months, but soon I was able to work that off at the stable.

When I was twelve or thirteen, I moved Snowflake to a private farm and paid board again. But eventually I wasn't there much. Right around the time I discovered horses in the fifth grade, I had started playing the violin. As I got older, I was staying home more, practicing. I joined the symphony orchestra in my town when I was only fifteen. I was finding it difficult to have two such strong interests—music and horses. But music was taking over in my life, so I let Snowflake go to a good home. I went on to study viola performance at the University of Michigan and Michigan State University, and I went to New York City to study under the world-famous violinist Joseph Fuchs of the Julliard School. Then I returned to my hometown to teach music and perform in the symphony.

Back home, I missed the presence of horses in my life and began shopping for one. When I got to the property where there were some prospects, I saw three tall, gorgeous horses in the field. I'm six foot three, so I wanted a tall horse. Two were bay horses—brown with a black mane and tail. The third was black with two white socks, a black mane, and a white tail. Oddly, he was named Silver.

When I went through the pasture gate, I was pleased that all three horses approached me. Suddenly I was a kid again, and like before, I stirred them up a little to see how they'd run. They took off at top speed with their tails in the air like flags. But Silver stood out to me. His head held high, his stride, the spring in his step, the general outline of the way he looked impressed me. In fact, I thought he was the most beautiful horse I'd ever seen. Plus he was the fastest of the three.

Silver was a three-year-old gelding, an Appendix quarter horse—a cross between a Thoroughbred, known for endurance and distance, and a quarter horse, the fastest of horses. Silver had the best of both worlds. My mare Snowflake had been a stable horse, "bomb-proof" and "broke to death" as horse people say about a predictable and child-safe horse. But I wasn't a child now. I wanted a horse I could train myself, and I decided Silver was the one for me. I bought him and boarded him outside of town.

Little did I know what I was getting myself into.

As I got to know Silver, I realized there was much more to this horse than I was used to. Having ridden predictable horses before, I didn't know they could be mischievous and arrogant—even bully-ish. I had not seen red flags when I bought Silver. I soon learned he was high-spirited and explosive. I would discover that one reason he was sold was his tendency to throw temper tantrums. He'd frightened the previous owner.

A couple of days after I bought Silver I could not catch him. I spent three and a half hours trying everything I could think of to coax him to come to me. I tried grain, treats, hay, even peppermints (catnip for horses). I finally gave up and went home, discouraged.

The next time, the landowner and her daughter joined me at the paddock. The landowner told me it wouldn't do any good to coax and trick Silver with treats. He needed a different incentive. The three of us positioned ourselves in a row in the middle of the paddock and gave Silver a chance to be caught. Instead he ran away.

The paddock was rectangular and about an acre. The landowner said, "We're going to keep him running." By waving lunge whips in the air, we kept Silver running around the paddock. Every ten minutes we'd stop, and I'd approach Silver to see if he was ready to come to me. When he wasn't, we kept him running. This went on for thirty or forty minutes. When he finally decided to be haltered, he was one tired and sweaty guy. I led him around to cool down and then gave him a nice grooming and spritz with the hose.

The next time I came to the paddock, I approached Silver with the halter. He ran away, so I kept the horse running by myself. It was successful, because finally when I approached Silver with a halter, he turned as if to run, then stopped as if he thought about it, then came directly to me. For a while Silver would come to me in the paddock without too much drama. The chapter of getting my horse to come to me was pretty much over.

Then came a new chapter: saddling and bridling. Silver had been ridden when I got him but by no means was he broke. I had to start from the beginning, and it took me a while to bridle and saddle him. Although I was being tutored by the landowner and her daughter, I was too tentative. I needed to be more confident. When the human is confident, the horse is confident. When the human is not, the horse is skittish and nervous. But I also had on my mind my uncle who was with me the first time I rode Silver in a round pen. Silver did just fine in those confines, and my uncle gave me this advice: "The main thing to remember is that constant love and attention will get him to come around."

This is true to a point, but I would have to learn the hard way that horses don't give you control or the leadership role. You can't beg it out of them. You can't treat it out of them. You have to take it, like they do in the field with each other every day. But in spite of the difficult early days of catching Silver, my uncle's advice was more appealing to me. I didn't want to be harsh with my horse. I wanted to love Silver through any problems.

I first truly understood that something was seriously wrong when I was riding with the landowner's daughter to one of the back fields. Silver would go to the beginning of the field but would not go forward. He began spinning around to go back to the barn. This was his first tantrum for me. The daughter was adamant. "No, Clyde, don't let him do that. Make him go forward. Don't let him bully you back to the barn. If he does it this once, he'll know he can do it anytime he wants."

Being so green, I asked what I should do. She offered a couple of techniques—grab the rein down by my knee, rein him into a circle, then let him out to go forward into the pasture. This worked until we got to the spot where he'd had his tantrum, and he had another one. We tried the technique again, but he'd already learned what I was going to do and was ready for it. When I tried to pull his head around a second time, he snatched the reins right out of my hand and reared straight up to a standing position. He almost went over backward. I was so taken aback I was almost paralyzed with fear, but I stayed on. Now I knew why he was sold.

Silver started back to the barn, and I tried reining him into a circle again. But he let me know I'd better stop or he'd explode once more. He stomped his hoof. We went back to the barn, and I lost the session that day. I hadn't learned how to fight, and I was still hopeful I wouldn't have to.

We abandoned the field for a while and went back to the round pen and paddock. I tried different techniques. I ran him in those spots, and when he was tired, I took him to the back field for rest. That worked once or twice—until it didn't. As soon as we got out in the big field, he'd become explosive again.

I intended to stay with it and with Silver. But for the next year and a half, it was up in the air as to who was training whom. The landowner told me Silver's brain was quick and he knew how to take advantage of a green rider. We went in the field only when Silver felt like it. Sometimes in the middle of a nice ride, he'd want to do something else—and would. Or he didn't want to go back to the paddock. He constantly changed his ways, but it all added up to Silver's being the boss.

One day I determined I would work through the tantrum. Sure enough, when I reined him around, Silver protested and reared straight up. I knew I could stay on, so I reined him around again. He reared up again. This went on for a while. I didn't realize that with all this rearing up, we were getting closer and closer to where Silver wanted to go—the barn. So he was still winning.

This was dangerous, not just for the rider but also for the horse. Twice when he reared up when I wasn't on him, he fell over backward. Luckily, he didn't get injured. Then the landowner said to me, "You'll never be able to take Silver to the back field, because he doesn't trust you. He doesn't trust that you'll keep him safe because you're not the leader."

I was floored. I could understand the logic, but I was still vague on how to become the leader. I was still trying to love Silver into submission, like my well-meaning uncle suggested. But it wasn't working. I had to start thinking fundamentally differently.

I got up the courage to reprimand Silver. I never had before. But I changed my attitude. There would be no more begging my horse to let me be the leader; I was taking control to become the leader. I saddled Silver up and put on a new bit. We rode around a little in the paddock so he could get the feel of the new bit, and I rubbed and touched him with a new thing—a riding crop.

That day I approached handling Silver like I would approach a difficult technical passage on the violin—viewing almost scientifically the mechanics of what's actually happening in that technique. I applied that way of thinking to Silver's rearing up and observed that, prior to his rearing, Silver would raise his head almost straight in the air. This made it impossible to rein him around, and soon he would rear. I had to stop that head-up behavior first; if he would keep his head down, he wouldn't rear up.

Sure enough, Silver started to put his head up. I tapped him very lightly on the poll (the top of his head), and his head came back down. We rode around the paddock. I motioned him to stop. Again, up with the head; again, I tapped him on the poll and the head went back down. About the sixth time, I saw him start to put his head up and then correct himself. He was learning. We ran through this three more times to be sure.

Time to go out in the field. There he did his usual shenanigans to go back to the barn, and this time, he did something new: he bucked. So I swatted his hindquarters with the crop, and his head went back up in the air. I reached back up and told him, "No, put your head down," and I tapped him on the poll again. His head came back down, but he bucked again. I repeated my behavior every time he misbehaved. We traveled down the lane back toward the barn like a see-saw. I could tell he was bewildered and did not want to go through this again. So I turned him back around and headed for the field. We got to his famous spot, and he acted like he wanted to turn around. But he actually shook his head as if to tell himself "no," and he kept going.

That day in the field, I could do anything with Silver. I could even start back to the barn, then turn around and go back to the field. I never had to fight with him again. We could actually enjoy each other's company. This was a turning point in Silver's life. He listened to me. He trusted me.

It was a turning point in my life too. I wanted to keep Silver, and I wanted to love my horse. I stayed dedicated to Silver during the hard stages. In a new and different way, this *was* what my uncle said—"constant love and attention will get him to come around." True. But I needed to be loving *and* firm. And it worked. Now I could show my love for my horse. And he reciprocated.

I remember my university music teacher giving a master class. A student was playing Brahms viola sonata in E-flat Major, which has a tempo and interpretation marking: *allegro amabile*. To play a lively *allegro*, the tempo needs to be almost risky. In this musical piece, the *amabile* means to give it a loving quality. The teacher drew our attention to *allegro amabile*, looked at the student, and said, "Sometimes loving can be risky." The student had played in a careful, timid way. But she needed courage to overcome the risk and play with flair and abandon. After that, she could bring out the loving quality of the piece more easily. That's what I needed to do with Silver, and I'm glad I took that risk.

I still have Silver. He's twelve years old as I write this. The black horse I found at three years old turned into a beautiful dapple-gray by age five and was pure white by age eight. These days I simply go to the field and call his name. He not only comes to me; sometimes he runs to me. He comes to the gate and "talks" to me—a low-pitched nicker. He's clearly glad to see me, and every time I leave, I receive a good-night nuzzle from him on my shoulder. I can ride Silver not only bareback but with no bridle—just a lead rope around the chest. I recently took him on a road ride bareback with just a rope halter.

Here's another thing. Silver doesn't tolerate bullying. When other horses fight in the field, Silver inserts himself in the middle and makes them stop. My fighting horse has become the pasture peacemaker.

Flash and the Mystery
of the Blue Hoof

Rachel Anne Ridge

R achel, you need to come to the barn and see something."
My husband, Tom, had a strange look on his face as he
opened the back door and called me away from the dishes. I
dried my hands on a towel and tried to read his expression.
Bewilderment? Amazement? Horror?

"What's going on?" I asked, slipping on my shoes and then
jogging behind him through the damp pasture to the three-
sided barn.

"I can't even . . . I don't know how to tell you this." Tom
stopped in his tracks and turned around to face me. I halted
and waited for details.

He inhaled. "Rach, there is something weird going on with
Flash."

Something weird with Flash? Flash was the stray donkey we'd adopted a few years earlier when he mysteriously showed up on our property, seemingly out of nowhere.

I thought back to the night he arrived. Exhausted and discouraged from a hard work day, we had just turned the car into our dirt driveway. It was late, and we couldn't wait to take warm showers, spend some much-needed time with our kids, and crawl into bed so we could forget about our problems. We'd been chasing our dream of making a living as artists, but a downturn in the economy had taken its toll, and we struggled to pay our bills. Worry clouded our minds and sapped our hope. And that's when we saw him standing in the middle of the road.

Tom slammed on the brakes. We sat and considered our options for a minute. Catching a scared donkey was about the last thing we felt like doing just then. We should just pass him by and forget we ever saw him. But then, with a sigh, we figured someone would be looking for him, and the least we could do was corral him.

We spent the next three hours trying to coax him into our pasture for overnight safekeeping.

It took every ounce of energy and ingenuity to bring the donkey in. He balked. He ran. He brayed. He sidestepped. He refused to budge. Inch by tedious inch, Tom finally got him inside the gate and chained it closed. It was a lot of trouble for a one-night stay, and by now, we couldn't wait to get rid of him.

In the morning we tried to find his owners by contacting the county sheriff, posting "Found Donkey" signs, and putting notices on bulletin boards in local feed stores. As luck would have it, that one night turned into two nights. Which turned into a week. Then two weeks. He was awfully cute, but we did not want to keep him. We did not want a donkey, thank you very much.

At least not at first.

You see, a family must think twice before adopting a five-hundred-pound animal with an appetite for everything in sight and a loud bray that can wake the neighbors. You don't just keep an equine you know nothing about, who appears to be an escape artist, and who refuses to cooperate with a lead rope. It's not a good idea to jump into donkey ownership without considering the implications.

Unless, that is, you start falling in love with him. Then it's a whole other story.

The shy donkey, with his deep scratches and gashes from his life on the lam, began to cast a spell over us. His long, dark eyelashes and tufted ears that turned like sonar dishes made him endearing. He was brownish-gray in color with small hooves and an oversized head, and his diminutive height was offset by his sturdy build. His bristly mane and wispy tail were connected by a chocolate stripe that rode down his back, which was crossed by another stripe over his narrow shoulders. And as he slowly allowed us to come close enough to dress his wounds and offer carrots, we began to see just how sweet-natured he was. His rubbery lips could express eagerness, hunger, sadness, and just plain old silliness. With each passing day, he relaxed into our temporary care and became a delightful part of our daily routine.

One day Tom started calling him "Flash," and just like that, the donkey's fate was sealed. He had found his forever home. And we became his forever owners. Because once you name a stray, it is yours. For keeps. Everyone else seemed to know this but us. And we fell right into donkey ownership, just like that.

"What's up with Flash?" I asked Tom now. In the years following Flash's adoption, he had been involved in numerous escapades. It was not unusual to find him messing with objects in the barn or making faces at the horses next door or eating twigs or rolling in a dust pile. I couldn't imagine what Tom meant by "something weird."

"He has a growth," Tom said slowly. "It's on his left front hoof, and it's hard as a rock."

"Okay . . . that sounds odd, but why are you shuddering?"

"Because . . ."—he paused—"it's blue. Bright blue."

"Whaaaaat?" I knew my expression was incredulous, but I instantly assumed Tom was playing some kind of joke on me.

"I'm not kidding," he said. "Come take a look." Tom led me to the barn, where Flash stood, quietly chewing on some hay. My eyes ran down his leg to his hoof . . . and there it was.

A bright blue bump. It ran around the outside of the hoof, like a ring, halfway up.

"I've inspected it and it's definitely some kind of growth." We pulled his hoof up to look at it. "It's attached like it just grew there overnight."

Like coral? *Hoof coral?*

I crouched with one knee on the ground. Yep, it was obviously part of his hoof, but how could it have appeared in one night out of nowhere? Was it a sign of some disease? A mineral deficiency? A health issue? Flash seemed fine, but then again, donkeys are such stoic creatures, maybe we didn't notice he was ill. This certainly could not be good.

Unless . . .

"Unless . . . ," Tom said thoughtfully, "unless it's some sort of sign."

Goosebumps tickled my arm at the thought. Now, I'm not normally a person who believes in "signs," but Tom gets these hunches sometimes that are uncanny. He has predicted tornadoes and major events throughout the years, so I usually pay pretty good attention when he thinks something's up. A blue hoof could be a sign of . . . a sign of . . . well, *what*?

Meanwhile, I Googled "blue hoof," "blue ring on hoof," "hoof disease," and anything else I could think of to get some answers, just in case it *wasn't* a supernatural sign. Surely, someone somewhere has had a donkey with a blue hoof.

I came up empty. No wiki-answers. No images of similar symptoms. No links to peculiar donkey diseases.

We kept a wary eye on that blue hoof. It was so bright and so odd, it was hard not to. We watched for any other strange symptoms but saw none. And just before I was about to call a vet to take a look at Flash's miraculous sign (to confirm it before going public), something else extraordinary happened.

It disappeared.

Vanished.

The blue growth was gone. Just like that.

Flash kept up his usual donkey antics—breaking into the barn, braying to the wind, fraternizing with the horses across the fence. Everything went back to normal for about three months, and then out of nowhere, it appeared again.

On the other hoof.

I froze when I saw it. Cold chills went up my spine. *What?* What could be the meaning of this?

I ran to the house and told Tom. "It's back. The blue growth is back, but this time it's on his other hoof!"

Tom dropped what he was doing and headed out to see for himself. We scratched our heads in wonder and creeped-out disbelief. "Strangest thing I've ever seen," he said as he turned to leave. "Face it, your donkey is weird."

Normally I'd be offended by such a statement, but for once I had to agree. This time, the blue hoof miracle only lasted a few days, and then it too was inexplicably gone, just as before. We pondered the meaning and looked for clues in the sky. I imagined crowds of people coming to pay homage to the humble donkey in Texas. Maybe Flash would be the answer to world conflict! Maybe he would bring hope to millions! Maybe he would end hunger and homelessness! I always knew he was special, but *this*! This was some kind of miracle.

Then suddenly, the answer came.

Tom came whistling up to the house with a funny grin. "I solved the mystery of the blue hoof," he said cockily. And with a flourish, he produced the ring itself from behind his back: a roll of blue painter's tape.

A ROLL OF PAINTER'S TAPE!

Bright blue, caked with mud, just the right size for a donkey hoof to step into and get stuck.

We looked at each other and burst out laughing. Mercy, I had to hold on to a chair to keep from falling over. Blue tape. Of course! Some random old roll of tape must have rolled onto the ground and Flash had managed to wedge a hoof into it—twice.

As the tears rolled down our cheeks, we thanked God Almighty that we hadn't called a vet to come take a look . . . or a newspaper to cover the story. Can you imagine how embarrassing that would have been? It seemed so obvious now, but at the time of the two miraculous blue ring appearances, we simply could *not* see what it was. We touched it, felt it, and tried to pry it away from the hoof, but it was on so tight that it appeared to be part of the hoof itself.

Oh, how we still laugh about the Blue Hoof Story. And each time we think of it, we are struck with the miracle. Not the miracle of the blue hoof, but the miracle of a stray donkey who arrived just when we needed a touch from above.

I pictured that first night with Flash once again. Catching a scared donkey was indeed the last thing we felt like doing. *Keeping* a donkey was the furthest thing from our minds.

It had taken hours to round up that animal and put him into our pasture. And when no one showed up to claim him, despite our best efforts to get rid of him, we opened our hearts, just a tiny bit, to consider letting him stay.

A stray donkey certainly didn't look like a miracle. But that floppy-eared, brown-eyed, shy animal made himself at home in our hearts and showed me that small miracles, everyday miracles, still happen. Just when I needed a respite from my worries, Flash appeared on our doorstep as comic relief. His antics, including his supernatural blue hoof, gave me daily reprieves and helped center my focus on simple delights I would have otherwise missed. Can a day really be so bad when a donkey is making faces at you with his lips? How can you be depressed when an offered cookie brings such joy to an eager friend? How can you resist rubbing fuzzy ears, even when all around you is chaos? And who could deny that scratching a donkey's butt, his favorite thing in the world, makes you feel better about life?

So maybe Flash's blue hoof wasn't a bona fide miracle. Maybe his name didn't make the headlines, and he didn't end world conflicts. Nobody came from far and wide to see the donkey with two scars across his nose, mementos of his previous life. But to me, Flash *himself* will always be a sign.

Flash is a reminder that miracles come in unexpected packages. Sometimes it takes getting out of the car and dragging them home. Sometimes it takes opening your eyes to the wonder of a bud about to blossom or a nest tucked into a crook in a tree. Sometimes they show up in the chatter around a dinner table, a warm pair of slippers, or a note in the mailbox. Sometimes the miracle looks like working your way through rough patches so you can follow your dream.

Oh, it would have been so easy to pass by the stray donkey and crawl into bed to forget about the worries of that day. But we would have missed the one thing we needed most.

We needed to open our hearts to the miracle of joy. To choose it. To not pass it by. Because when we do, we realize joy is already around us, ready to transcend our circumstances and transform our thinking.

Just like that stray donkey did—the one with a blue hoof.

The Legend of the Donkey's Cross

Donkeys come in many different colors—black, dark brown, gray, spotted, and white. Most have distinct markings called "light points," or white muzzles and rings around their eyes, as well as a "cross" on their backs. The cross is made by a dark brown or black dorsal stripe that runs from the withers and down the tail, which is intersected by a stripe across the withers that extends down each shoulder. Legend has it that Jesus rewarded the donkey for his loyalty to him when he carried Jesus into Jerusalem and remained with him at the crucifixion. It is said that the shadow of the cross fell across the donkey's back and remained there as a tribute to the importance of God's humblest of creatures.

—Rachel Anne Ridge

Dynamite

Sherri Gallagher

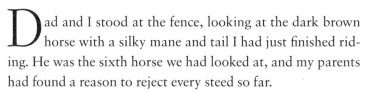

D ad and I stood at the fence, looking at the dark brown horse with a silky mane and tail I had just finished riding. He was the sixth horse we had looked at, and my parents had found a reason to reject every steed so far.

"I really like this one, Dad. He's just the right size for me."

Dad shook his head. "No, he's too small. If we're going to get a horse, I want something I can ride too."

I was fourteen years old. This was the third year in a row I had worked for my parents all summer and not been paid a penny because they said they would buy me a horse in the fall. Then fall would come and it seemed there was always a reason not to buy a horse. Once winter closed in they would say it was too late, and they would get the horse for me "next year." The next year would roll around and the promise forgotten as we went through the same routine once again. I was more than frustrated. I was angry. The thing that kept me going was riding my friend Cheryl's horses, but I wanted a horse of my own.

I turned and slammed my way into the backseat of the car, tears streaming down my face. I had held up my end of the bargain, but it looked like Mom and Dad didn't plan on holding up theirs. They took their seats in the front, and we rode home in silence. As soon as the car stopped I escaped to my room, blinking away tears as I worked out algebra problems.

The door opened and closed softly, and Mom took a seat on my bed. She waited. I ignored her. "I know you're disappointed. But your Dad has a point. If we are going to the expense of buying a horse, it needs to be one the whole family can ride."

I wrote the answer to the current problem and started to copy the next one, not bothering to look at Mom. "You don't know how to ride," I reminded her, "and Dad hasn't ridden since he was a teenager. This is just another excuse so I can't have a horse."

Mom heaved a deep sigh. "I promise you, if you can find a horse that both of you can ride, is healthy, and in our price range, we will buy it."

Mom left as quietly as she had arrived. As soon as I heard the door shut, I pulled the well-read and carefully marked newspaper from my stack of books. There was only one ad left that I hadn't called on. At my friend Cheryl's suggestion, I had been watching for horses owned by girls going off to college; they were the most likely to be well cared for and trained, with the right home being more important than the purchase price.

This notice was a whole different situation. A stable owner was moving to Florida and selling off his excess stock. All sales were final and had to be completed by Wednesday. Taking a deep breath, I went to the living room where Mom and Dad watched television.

"There is one more number to call, but we will have to go tomorrow night as soon as we get home and make a decision," I announced.

"Okay, we can do that," Dad answered, "but don't get your hopes up. I'm not buying just any horse because you're having a temper tantrum." And with that, he turned back to his program.

I called and made the arrangements. Then a quick call to Cheryl, my resource for all things to do with horses, and she was up for the visit.

The next day school dragged on for an eternity while the wind gusted and the gray sky dripped rain the weatherman promised would be snow by the weekend. I rushed through my evening chores and homework as I waited for my parents to arrive home from work. By the time we had collected Cheryl and gotten to the stables, the light had left the sky and twilight was descending.

The stable owner wore a cowboy hat and had white hair and a mustache. Bundled against the weather, he nodded to us and spoke to my parents while Cheryl and I wandered through the barn trying to pick out the right horse to buy.

The man called out, "So, young lady, you want to buy a horse."

"Yes, sir. Are all of these for sale?" I motioned to the full stalls.

"Nope. These are going to Florida with me. I got one horse left to sell, and he's up back in the pasture. I'll go git 'em." With that he tightened the cinch on a nondescript Appaloosa and rode out.

We waited in silence. The slow clip-clop of hooves got louder and faster until a big palomino trotted into the aisle, down between a few stalls, and straight into the grain bin. The cowboy appeared a few seconds later, leaping out of the saddle in a manner that would have made John Wayne proud. "I should have known. Dynamite, git outta there."

A quick grab and slamming of the bin lid and the horse backed out and into an empty stall.

"He's a good horse and trail savvy. You won't have no problems with him."

I looked at the horse calmly nibbling hay and climbed the stall boards to lean in with a peppermint candy. He took it with gentle lips and snuffled against the sleeve of my wool coat before returning to the hay.

"Suppose you want to ride him."

"Yes, please."

"We'll have to come back on the weekend for you to do that," Dad said. "It's too dark to do that safely now."

"Ain't no problem," the cowboy said. "I got lights. This ain't no spooky horse. Shadows won't set him off." He swung a saddle into place. Dynamite grabbed another mouthful of hay as a straight snaffle bit was tucked into his mouth, and he was led outside to the parking lot.

I walked over to his left shoulder and realized I couldn't see over Dynamite's back. As a matter of fact I had to look up to even see his back. Well, Dad couldn't claim this one was too small for him.

The cowboy laced his fingers and bent down so I could step into the loop they made. "Up you go."

I was in the saddle. The stirrups were set for an adult, but that wasn't a problem. I clung with my knees and reined Dynamite about. A few kicks achieved a slow trot, but that was the extent of the speed I could get out of him. I glanced at Cheryl. She made a circle of her thumb and forefinger, signaling okay.

I stopped him in front of my parents. "Do you want to ride him, Dad?"

Boxed into a corner, Dad said, "Sure."

I slid down the side of the horse, leaning against his warm bulk until my legs, which shook with excitement, would hold me, and handed over the reins. Dad took a deep breath and climbed up. Dynamite continued to chew the hay wrapped around the bit. Dad walked the horse through some right and left circles and came back and handed over the reins. "He seems like a nice enough horse. What do you want for him?"

The old cowboy squinted and looked at me and then at Dad. "A hunnerd and fifty dollars."

I wasn't sure if it was a trick of the lights or if Dad's face paled. He had given me the go-ahead for any horse up to $500—so he couldn't reject Dynamite for price either. "That's reasonable, but we don't have a way to transport him home, so I don't think we can do this."

The cowboy rubbed the stubble around his mouth. "Well, I'm delivering all the sold horses on Thursday. You give me directions, and I'll drop him off, no charge."

Mom and Dad exchanged looks.

"That's very nice of you, but we don't have a saddle or any equipment to ride him," Dad said.

The old cowboy crossed his arms. "I'll throw in a saddle and bridle and halter. Anything else?"

Mom stepped forward. "Can you deliver him next week? We have to put up fencing and won't get to it until the weekend."

The cowboy started to shake his head no, and a look of relief crossed my parents' faces until Cheryl piped up. "That won't be a problem. Sher and I can get your field fenced with barbed wire in a day. We've got a teacher institution day on Wednesday."

I took the cue and jumped in. "Cheryl can come home with me on Tuesday after school, and we can get right to work first thing Wednesday morning. We can stop at the feed mill on the way home tonight and buy the stuff."

Mom and Dad were speechless. The old cowboy turned and tugged one of the curls that had escaped my winter hat, a smile dancing on his lips. "Looks like you got yerself a horse there, little lady."

Dynamite was mine.

Installing barbed wire fencing turned out to be fairly easy, if you didn't mind getting poked with the barbs. Most of the field was lined with sturdy trees, and we would run the spool out about ten feet. Cheryl would grab the wire near a barb and pull it tight while I hammered in the staples. The only problem was the fence near the house where there were no trees. Our house was built on the knob of a hill and the Onondaga limestone came within a few inches of the surface. We were only able to sink the fence posts about a foot into the soil before hitting stone—that line definitely wobbled. Dad deemed it acceptable and built a one-horse shelter.

Dynamite arrived the next night and, after a dinner of sweet feed and a big pile of hay, settled in to sleep. I was up early to feed him before school, having slept with his saddle resting on the footboard of my bed and hugging his bridle. Charging home from school I would saddle up and ride or just sit in the pasture near him while he grazed.

Dynamite was a calm fellow with feet the size of pie plates and a sense of humor. And he was fun. Unfortunately, my Dad was a heavy smoker and always had a pack of cigarettes in his pocket. About two weeks after Dynamite arrived, Dad crossed the fence into the pasture. Dynamite was there immediately, snuffling my father intently. Dad gave him a shove, but Dynamite just kind of rolled with the shove and then rolled right back, rubbing his head against the human scratching post. Dad gave in and started rubbing under the halter in those places a horse just can't get to. That was all it took; Dynamite snatched the cigarettes out of Dad's pocket in a heartbeat and trotted off across the pasture while Dad alternately laughed and called my horse names. He watched helplessly as Dynamite chowed down on the tobacco, paper and all. Dad was more careful after that.

About a month into having a horse, the novelty wore off, and like a typical teenager, I slept in—or tried to anyway. My relaxed slumber was interrupted when my mother slammed open my bedroom door. "Get up."

I buried my head under the pillow, "Okay, just a few more minutes."

"Get up now." A few seconds later the blankets sailed through the air to land in a heap on the floor.

I jumped out of bed and grabbed a robe, shivering. "I'm up."

"Go to the kitchen. Now."

The stairs opened into the kitchen, a sheltered window lighting the last step. As I came down the stairs, very little light came through the glass. Now I understood Mom's problem. Dynamite had escaped the pasture by putting his head under that wobbly line of fencing and lifting the whole thing out of the ground, posts and all. He now stood with his rear end pressed against the kitchen window, waiting for me to appear with his breakfast. So much for sleeping in—for the next four years.

As is usual in the Syracuse, New York, area, heavy snowfalls landed and stayed, piling into huge drifts. Riding was difficult then. By winter break the roads were canyons with snow walls well over a rider's head, even on a big horse like Dynamite, and the fields drifted over. Deciding to risk it, one day I saddled Dynamite and headed up the road. My placid, sleepy horse had his head up, ears swiveling, and was blowing large noisy snorts of steamy breath. He danced in place and kept spinning to head back to his pasture.

"Cut it out, you chucklehead," I chided. "We won't be out long."

By the time we reached the top of the steep section, I was sweating, and so was my horse. I turned the reins to head up a little-used farm road. Dynamite stopped and refused to move. I kicked and clucked and swatted his rear, all to no avail. When your horse is a solid twelve to fourteen hundred pounds and your own weight hasn't broken into triple digits yet, winning a battle of wills is difficult. I stopped to catch my breath, trying to figure out how to make my horse do what I wanted without being mean.

A movement in the hedge lining the road caught my eye. I recognized a coydog creeping closer to the edge of the farm road through the tangle of brush the animal used to mask his approach. My hands turned to ice, and it had nothing to do with the air temperature. We were in trouble. Coydogs are a cross between a domestic dog and a coyote. Where coyotes would normally avoid humans, the domestic dogs that joined the pack had no fear of man. Gone completely feral, they had no reservations about attacking anything, including people.

I turned Dynamite for home. He took off in a fast trot down the steep, icy road while I held my breath and worked at remaining balanced on his shoulders. If he went down, broken bones would be the least of my worries. As we turned into the driveway, I glanced back up the road to see a pack of over thirty coydogs massed where we had stopped. If it hadn't been for

Dynamite's sharp senses, I would have ridden us into a situation neither of us would have survived. Needless to say, Dynamite spent the rest of the winter in the garage instead of his pasture.

Summer eventually came, and the coydogs had plenty of natural food, so it was safe for a horse to be outside. It was a warm day, not a cloud in the sky and only a light summer breeze to keep the flies away. I tied Dynamite to an apple tree and let him munch his fill. As dusk settled in I went to put him back in the pasture.

My dad stepped out onto the stoop. "Leave him there for the night. The grass is better there. He'll be fine."

I went in for supper and checked my horse before going to bed. Dynamite stood, head down asleep, his rump tucked against the tree trunk.

When Mom rose the next morning she found him wound around the tree. Mom was more than a little scared of my big horse, but she courageously decided to help him. Wearing a bathrobe and slippers, she picked up a doughnut, showed it to Dynamite, and began walking around the tree to unwind him. Of course wanting the treat, the horse hurried to catch up to my mother. The feel of his hot breath on the top of her head frightened her, so she began to jog. Dynamite began a slow trot. Mom started to run, screaming for help but still circling the tree. Dad and I hot-footed it outside to see Mom, in bathrobe and slippers, running as fast as she could with Dynamite trotting along behind her.

Dad yelled, "Drop the doughnut!"

Mom threw the treat to the ground and continued to run, still in a circle around the tree. Dynamite stopped to eat. Dad and I fell to the ground laughing, tears running down our faces. Without Dynamite breathing down her neck, Mom was able to think and hurried back to the house. She paused for a moment to look at Dad and me lying on the ground.

"You two are a lot of help," she snapped, and then stomped into the house. It was enough to set Dad and me back laughing for several more minutes.

Dynamite was a great kid's horse, ever steady and reliable. I could stand in his saddle and pick apples and pears. He followed me around like my German Shepherds. I never had to worry about him running away with me, and I could ride him with a rope and halter or saddle and bridle. He was the perfect companion for a lonely, four-eyed misfit with only one friend and no close neighbors.

When it came time to leave for college, I knew Dynamite wouldn't be happy alone. In all sadness I gave him to a family with two young boys. The day they came to take him away, he whinnied for me as the trailer went up the road. I cried great sobs, but it was the best thing for him. I received pictures of Dynamite with both boys up top or all three swimming in a pond. He had a clean, shiny coat and well-fed belly, and I knew he was happier with his children to play with than he would be alone in my parents' yard.

Many of the things I did with Dynamite were the things you shouldn't do with a horse: keeping him alone with no herd and only a teenage girl, letting him eat tobacco and doughnuts, tying him to a tree. Each of those things had caused the death of other horses. Thankfully, Dynamite was the right horse to take it all in stride and carry his child rider through the ups and downs of growing up.

Safety

Katy Pistole

My family had recently moved to the booming town of Bumpass in the countryside of Central Virginia. I was living my dream of having my beloved horses in my backyard. I could look out any window and see them grazing or hanging out in the run-in shed.

Scooter, my little red horse I'd rescued several years earlier, had come a long way. He no longer viewed me as his enemy but as a trusted friend and leader.

One of the first signs of Scooter's trust came with flies. Flies may seem like a small annoyance to humans, but to horses they are a genuine source of fear. Blood-sucking species like greenheads and cow flies literally drill their needle-like mouths into the blood-rich skin of horses. The fly's favorite drill sites are the croup (top of the rump) and between the back legs, high up, where the sheath or teats are. Both places are difficult for horses to reach.

These flies are hard to kill and may zoom off even after being slapped. If you are going to kill them, you must hit hard. I hate flies and the torture they exact on my horses. But the flies serve an interesting purpose. They are a barometer for relationship.

As much as I hate flies and what they do to Scooter, if I begin slapping before he trusts my heart, he will be unable to experience relief from pain. He will think I am slapping *him*. So I wait for the flies to do their work. I wait for the flies to create a need. I don't enjoy Scooter's pain, but I want his participation in the fly killing.

A couple of years after I rescued him, Scooter recognized my ability to kill the flies. He would stand still for me to wave flies from his face. Then he could stand for me to push them away from his hindquarters. Then came the day I'd waited for.

He trotted to me and presented his rear end, asking for my help with a large cow fly. I slapped carefully, my hand cupped to minimize the impact on Scooter. The fly dropped to the ground, and I stomped on it, twisting my foot to mash it into the dirt. Scooter sniffed the crushed bug and took a step closer to me.

He began seeking me, to present the bug on him so I could squash it. And I had to slap really hard. But Scooter knows my heart, and so we are allies in a war against the things that hurt him, things that disturb his safety.

Horses need safety, and the primary responsibility of the leader is to provide safety for the herd. Scooter found that need met in me and viewed himself as the leader of my small herd of four.

Louisa County is mostly farmland and forest, and we were aware that large predators roamed freely. We had even seen signs of bear scat in the pasture. While a bear is not likely to bring down a healthy horse, my old horse Dreamsicle could be a target if a bear ever came hunting on my property.

One morning I heard my twelve-year-old daughter shriek. "*Mom*! There's a bear in the pasture and it's chasing the horses!"

I rushed to the kitchen window and, sure enough, what looked like a small black bear was attacking Scooter. The horse alternately ran toward and away from the creature, drawing it from the herd. The other three horses raced in circles, screaming and snorting, heads high with terrified vigilance.

A second bear joined the chase, and Scooter kicked out and ran faster.

When I looked harder, I realized the animals were not bears, but two huge Rottweilers. I grabbed the phone book and looked up Animal Control. My hand shook so hard I had trouble pushing the buttons. The casual voice on the other end assured me this was not something they could attend to, and that I was free to shoot the offending dogs.

Great.

I handed the phone to my daughter, who seemed glued to her spot at the window. "Listen to me!"

She dragged her eyes from the scene in the pasture.

"Take this." I handed her the phone. "Stay here—do *not* come outside, no matter what happens. If anything does happen, call 9-1-1."

She gulped and nodded, staring at the buttons on the phone, then into my face, her eyes full of tears ready to spill.

I grabbed my son's aluminum base-ball bat and sprinted toward the

melee. Adrenaline surged through my veins, and I ran faster—consciously focusing my glare on one of the attacking dogs. I must have looked serious, because the second dog stopped chasing and stared at me momentarily before turning and retreating up the hill toward the road.

The other dog, though, whirled around to face me.

I was familiar with body language, and this dog looked scary. Her head down, brown eyes locked on mine, hackles up, teeth showing.

But don't mess with my Scooter—or any of my horses.

I positioned my bat and prepared to swing. I did not want to hurt the dog, but I would if necessary. She approached with the slow, stiff-legged hostility of an aggressive predator.

I was ready. I didn't want to swing too soon, or I would leave myself vulnerable to attack. She needed to get just a little closer. Soon I could see the tartar on her teeth, and I hunkered down, closing my fingers firmly on the throat of the bat.

Suddenly the dog stopped. Her head came up, and her eyes grew wide and unfocused. She seemed to be staring over my left shoulder. And she looked confused.

I remained ready, rocking left to right.

The dog licked her lips and glanced to her left, in the same direction the other dog ran. Before I could make sense of what was happening, she turned and jogged away, up the hill toward the road. Just as she reached the creek, she turned and looked at me once more, then leaped across the creek and trotted away.

I straightened slowly and wondered what on earth had happened.

A soft muzzle snuffled at my hair, and I turned around.

All four horses had lined up, shoulder to shoulder, directly behind me.

They were not there to protect me. They were there because I am their protection. Scooter had brought his herd to the safest place in the pasture.

Me.

Tears stung my eyes as I wrapped my arms around Scooter's sweet neck. He tucked his chin, pressing into my back.

Safety. It's what horses need.

The Art of the Whoa

Sarah Parshall Perry

I'd like to avoid all the clichés about horse-crazy little girls, with their Breyer horse models and their horse posters, their stuffed horses and shelves of horse books. But I can't, because I was the perfect embodiment of that cliché.

It may be that such a description is a rite of passage for girls who love animals. I do remember that my sister and I—a mere year and a half apart in age—argued once about who got to pick the horse as their favorite animal, as if there were some unspoken rule between us that, competitive as we were, we could not both love the same thing. So I demanded—er, *suggested*—she pick the deer as her favorite animal instead of the horse. They looked passably similar, I thought. Four legs, big eyes, large, twitchy ears. I sold her on something like, "Look how beautiful and graceful they are! Don't you want one?" (Because, you know, *plenty* of people have pet deer.)

My sister bought this paltry ruse, and subsequently horses were "mine." Though I must say this self-selection was a bigger drain on my parents than it was on me. Turns out, it's kind of hard to get one daughter the book *Black Beauty* for Christmas and find a matching gift for the other. Once you've given her *The Yearling*, you're pretty much out of luck.

The next natural request on my part was for a pony. And riding lessons. I got the latter. For a little while.

The former came to me thirty years, a husband, three kids, a job, and a mortgage later.

After graduate school, when I was entrenched in the real (to wit: non-academic, non-sleeping-until-your-first-class-at-noon) world, all my juvenile equine daydreams came racing back. No matter what it took, I was going to ride—in my "free time," of course, when I'm not knee-deep in sibling arguments and stinking laundry. This means every minute at the barn is a minute hard-fought and precious, which shows how much I love my horse and our sport. It shows how hard I'm willing to work at the thing I had to wait what seemed like forever to get.

I had started in Western lessons as a kid. This pretty much consisted of my one-eyed "trainer" (note the quotation marks) laughing as I tried to haul the twenty-five-pound saddle to the barn aisle, and later silently leaning over the ring with crossed arms as I cantered around a dusty circle and tried to catch a glimpse of myself in the far-side mirror. "Silently," as in my dad was paying him to watch me ride, something he could have done for free himself. I am pretty sure "training" also requires "speaking."

I am awesome! I thought as I sailed around the ring, long hair billowing behind me like a flag.

I was wrong.

Many years later when I took up riding again, I bounced from barn to barn the first few years and tried to relearn (i.e., start from total scratch with a host of embarrassing gaffes relative to technique, terms, and form) the pursuit of English riding—the thing that is part science, part art, part sport, part silent pleading with God that you don't end up in the dirt on the backside of an oxer when you miss the distance to your jump.

But my equine partners were never mine. They were borrowed or leased. They were loved and let go, and I came to my husband more often than he cares to recall with the same whine: "I'm never going to get my own horse!"

"In riding a horse, we borrow freedom."

HELEN THOMPSON

The eight-year-old girl with pigtails and a room full of horse toys was back with a vengeance. Indeed she had never really left, but had hung in the wings of an unfolding life, patiently waiting through years of school, boyfriends, and relocations for an opportunity to go back to asking the same question. Very, very loudly. It so happens that my desire for a horse was actually the thing I had wanted more and for longer than anything else in the world. Not a house of my own, not a dazzling professional career. Not a husband or children. Actually, don't tell them about that last part. I'm not sure they know.

Then, after my thirty-eighth birthday, my husband gave me a budget and a green light. After hours on the computer trolling the classifieds, go-sees, and trial rides, and praying that "my" horse would find me, I discovered a tall, plain bay less than an hour from my house and from my trainer's barn.

His name was Stuart. Nothing fancy, like The Governor or Sapphire. Nothing that screamed marquee champion, like Baloubet du Rouet or Portofino 63. He had the name of the kid who would have tied your braids to your chair in kindergarten. I had sought white markings. He hadn't a speck on him. I had prayed for a show hunter. He was trained in the jumpers. I had wanted an affectionate cuddle-bug. He couldn't stand to be snuggled, and to this day, will only approach me first if he knows I have a treat. The blanket he came with had "trouble" written on the side in silver electrical tape. This should have been my first clue that this relationship of ours was something I would have to work at. And maybe also, just plain survive.

But this Stuart of mine—my tall, plain bay—can jump the moon. And he is as honest as they get. Which is to say he doesn't run out from the approach to a fence, or slam on the brakes, or rear when you happen to hit him in the mouth on those instances that your hands haven't caught up with your body and you simultaneously tell your horse to "go" *and* "whoa" at the same time, something that would make anyone crazy but especially a twelve-hundred-pound animal whose natural instinct is to run.

This is particularly kind of him, as I am one of the older riders in our barn, and with three children underfoot, I do suspect Stuart somehow knows he cannot go breaking me whenever he wants, because there are little people counting on me.

I've been at this riding thing about eleven years, with breaks for childbirth and illnesses and travel in between. But only the last two years of my life have been shared with Stuart (now named Caspian as far as the horse show judges are concerned). I've had a few successes in the show ring, but I'm not anywhere close to the goals I've set for myself. This might be the result of how hard I've been working at riding. That is, very, very hard.

I am one of the most doggedly determined women you'll meet. My vices are many, but sloth is not among them. If I set out to fold laundry on Monday, then by 11:59 p.m. on Monday night I might be folding the fourteen hundredth sock pair, but the task—tornado or missing limb notwithstanding—will have been completed. I am the same woman who took twenty-two credits a semester in college to graduate early, then studied nearly three hundred hours for the bar exam. I'm fairly awesome at self-flagellation, so it's unspeakably frustrating to have so many "disagreements" with both my horse and trainer during a lesson, or completely miss a rudimentary element in the show ring. Unless I'm actually working *too* hard. It can be a challenge to get out of my own way.

A few weeks ago I came into the barn with my guard up. Stuart had had five days off. This is a potential nightmare for the owner of a fit, young Thoroughbred. Time off + excellent fitness + breeding for speed = rapid, hooved acceleration. And, I'm convinced, a rather selfish death wish for his owner, considering I'm the one who pays his bills.

I needed to confirm for both of us that I was in control. But the harder I worked on perfect form, the more I tried to do Stuart's job for him, the more aggressive I was, the more agitated he became until everything fell apart. I jumped up his neck too early in anticipating the jumps, and I didn't recover in enough time on the back end to make him straight and steady. He kicked out, and I pulled back, and then he dropped his head and nearly yanked me out of the tack and onto the ground in an effort to get the bit between his teeth and take me for a spin. At one point we were nearly cantering in place, each of us tugging the bit away from the other. I imagined my guardian angel needed a cocktail after the whole sweaty fiasco. My trainer kept repeating (read: hollering), "You need to trust him and stop overdoing it! Set him up to the jump, and just let him go!"

Oh, you mean, work a little less and trust a little more?

As if the Lord was giving me a direct speech because he needed an obvious metaphor for someone who is fairly set in her ways. Like if I had just loosened up, things might have turned around.

This is not as easy as my trainer thinks. It's certainly not as easy as Stuart thinks. In fact, I'm sure when he's in his roomy stall, cross-ventilated with windows that open to a field of knee-high timothy and gabbling chickens, his only thought (if any exists) is, "I wish that crazy mother who gets on my back four times a week would just lighten up already! I should dump her just to teach her . . . ooh! Dinner!"

Opening my hand on the things I love, this willingness to do what I can and then release the results, has always been hard. The more I love something, the more likely I am to suffocate it with a death grip. I am excellent at the striving part. I am quite weak at the letting go part. Like all that initiative and ardency are going to work to my benefit and actually bring the thing I want to fruition. So if I am ultimately blessed with that thing I want, I leave so little time to experience the simple joy of being with it—of being with Stuart.

In his own way, Stuart's petulance in the ring, his "one of these days I will dump you if you keep working so hard" attitude, has forced me to settle myself and slow the pace. And, as horses are wont to do, he teaches me this lesson in riding and in life. I remember why it is I so badly wanted a horse not only when we are champion in our division, but more often when the barn is quiet and I towel-dry his legs in the wash stall and comb the mane that refuses to lay flat. When I stroke his face where a star might have been, between two kind eyes, the ones that always look as though they are asking me something. When his head lowers and his breath slows and the barn swallows dart above us, I put my head on his dark neck and breathe deeply as I practice the art of the whoa.

Whop!

Rebecca E. Ondov

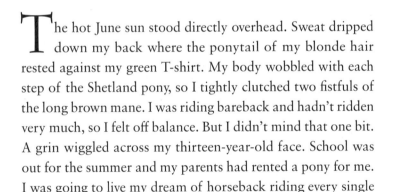

The hot June sun stood directly overhead. Sweat dripped down my back where the ponytail of my blonde hair rested against my green T-shirt. My body wobbled with each step of the Shetland pony, so I tightly clutched two fistfuls of the long brown mane. I was riding bareback and hadn't ridden very much, so I felt off balance. But I didn't mind that one bit. A grin wiggled across my thirteen-year-old face. School was out for the summer and my parents had rented a pony for me. I was going to live my dream of horseback riding every single day. I had no idea what was in store for me.

The pony's hooves clopped on the dirt path that rimmed the fields of the tall stalks of corn, which stretched in front of us, row after row across the southern Minnesota countryside. I could ride for miles and never come to a fence. I wanted to race down the path with the wind in my face and feel like I was flying. My heart thumped wildly as I gathered the reins, leaned forward, and nudged the mare's sides to urge her forward. Nothing happened. *Maybe she doesn't understand. After all, she has had a lot of other kids ride her.*

I snuggled deeper into the hollow of the mare's back. Her brown hair prickled my bare legs where the fabric of my shorts ended. Leaning forward, I kicked with both legs. But the mare merely plodded down the path. I thumped my legs against her side. She dawdled along. Pumping my legs, I whined, "C'mon, Y-Butt. You're supposed to run." But the pony merely turned her head and squinted at me.

I gritted my teeth and gathered the reins with a clump of mane in my left hand. In my right hand I grasped the ends of the reins and swatted her rear end with them. She jumped. I swayed off balance. Clinging to her mane, I centered myself as she trotted a few seat-jarring steps, then once again settled into a walk. I growled, "That's not what I wanted. And you know it."

Gripping her sides with my long and gangly legs, I whacked her with the reins. The little brown-and-white mare shot forward like a bullet. I hung on for dear life as the muggy air pelted my face. Suddenly her front end buckled as she dropped to her knees and skidded to a stop. I sailed over her head. Whop! I smashed into the ground. The wind was driven out of me. I lay there for a few moments, trying to catch my breath while listening to the mare pluck long stems of green grass. I wondered, *What happened? Could she have hurt her legs?* Instantly I felt bad for whacking her with the reins.

After brushing myself off, I walked over to the mare. "Are you okay?" I ran my hand down her legs and picked up each foot. Nothing seemed to be wrong. *I don't know much about horses. What if something is wrong? I don't want to hurt her.* I patted her neck. "Okay, girl, I'll walk you home just to make sure."

When I led the mare down the driveway of the pasture where I kept her, Duane, the farm owner, was working in the yard. He stopped and asked, "Is everything okay?" I shrugged and explained. He merely chuckled. "That pony is fine. She did that because she's lazy and didn't want to run. Don't let her get away with that again." I nodded and quickly led the mare away so Duane couldn't see me blush. My mind raced. The pony had probably done this to dozens of kids. Maybe she was even laughing at me as I sailed over her head. When I turned her loose in the pasture I scowled and wondered, *Is this what it's like to own a horse?*

All my life I'd dreamt of owning a horse. I'm sure if you examined my DNA you'd discover God tucked the horse-crazy gene in it. Nearly from conception I'd begged and pleaded with my parents to buy me *my very own horse*, but my dad was just starting to build his professional life and Mom was a stay-at-home mother for us three kids. We lived in a small home. They didn't have money to spare. Besides, they were raised during the Great Depression, so even spending money on food was an incredible investment. But a horse? It didn't help matters that we lived in town. Their response was always the same: "Where would you keep a horse?" I'd shrug my shoulders, wait a few days, then plead some more.

I hadn't made any headway with them until seventh grade. My new best friend owned horses. I'm sure my cheeks were flushed with excitement when I stepped inside the back door after horseback riding with her. Later that year they finally succumbed to my begging and had scraped together enough money to rent a pony for the summer. I nodded my head while they explained that, since it was my dream, I would have to be the one to take care of the pony, and it was up to me to find a way to get out to the pasture. There was no money for a saddle, so I'd have to ride bareback.

The rest of that spring droned past as I sat in classes waiting for school to be over. I'd stare out the window and imagine myself horseback riding every day all summer—my dream was coming true! That's what I thought—but that was before my first ride on that dream pony.

The day the rusty horse trailer dropped off the plump brown-and-white paint pony, I stood in the farm yard. My heart nearly melted with excitement. The man explained that the mare's name was Y-Butt. He pointed to her mostly chocolate-brown rear end, which had a big blotch of white hair on it that looked like a "Y."

After the man drove away I brushed my pony down, buckled her bridle in place, and led her to a stump so I could use it as a step stool and slip onto her back. My emotions fluttered as I gathered the reins and nudged her down the driveway. I teetered, unbalanced, as she walked a few steps, then stopped. Nicely, I squeezed my legs. Nothing. I kicked. She didn't even flinch. So I thumped her sides, but she refused to budge. I was embarrassed when I glanced up and saw Duane watching out his kitchen window. Finally I lifted my legs away from her side and with all my energy I kicked her. The pony backed up!

Duane cracked the back door open and yelled over to me, "She's barn sour. Do you want some help?" I nodded and was glad I did. After he hopped on, it took him half an hour to get her to walk the hundred feet out the driveway. That's why, days later, when I walked into the driveway leading the mare, he said the mare was lazy. He had it figured out. The mare had snookered me again! Y-Butt was really a monster disguised as a pony.

Whop!

The following day as I pedaled my bike the three miles to the pasture, I rehearsed in my mind what I would do. I was determined that pony was not going to get the best of me. Once again the hot sun beat down on me as I rode the trail next to the rows of corn. Y-Butt refused to speed up until I whacked her, but this time I was ready. Whack! She shot forward like a rocket. When she dropped to her knees I quickly whacked her again. Instantly she sprang to her feet and continued to lope along the trail.

I smiled. Momentarily. Suddenly she swerved ninety degrees, launching me into the air. Whop! I smashed into the ground and couldn't breathe. I glanced at the pony. Y-Butt scarfed down the green grass like she hadn't eaten in a week, but she was watching me out of the corners of her big brown eyes.

Each day she had a new tactic for how to help me dismount. It was a good thing I was riding bareback so I didn't get hung up in the saddle when I flew off. She was an old hand at this and knew every trick in the book. Every summer she got a new kid to buffalo. The worst trick was when she'd grab the bit in her teeth and run. Even though I'd pull as hard as I could, I couldn't pry the bit loose. She'd race forward like a freight train, then stop or turn suddenly. One time she ran straight for the barbed wire fence. My heart pounded as I envisioned us being tangled up and the pony getting cut by the razor-sharp wire. But at the last moment she put on the skids and stopped in the nick of time. I sailed over the top. Whop! Another time she raced through the woods to a branch that was too low for me to duck underneath. Whop! The bruises on my body didn't hurt nearly as badly as the bruises in my heart.

One morning as I slowly pedaled my bike toward the pasture, the weight of discouragement was nearly too heavy to bear.

This didn't look anything like my dream. It was too hard. I was ready to tell my parents to have the guy come pick up this nasty little horse. I sighed and chewed on my lip. Tears dripped down my face. *If I quit now, Dad and Mom will not give me another chance.* When I thought about never owning my very own horse, my heart shivered. That thought felt like a death sentence to my spirit. I whispered a small prayer.

After brushing Y-Butt and buckling the bridle in place, I led her next to the stump and slipped onto her back. She sauntered down the driveway, and my mind drifted over all the wrecks I'd had and what a rotten pony she was. I blamed her all the way down the dirt road, through the woods, and around the cornfield. I blamed her for all my bruises, for ruining my summer, and for messing up my dream.

A light breeze rustled the tall stalks of corn. Her hooves clopped on the dirt path. I gathered the reins and leaned forward before I would kick her into a lope. As I tucked my chin to brace myself, I noticed Y-Butt flattened her ears. *That's weird.* I leaned backward to my normal riding position, and her ears pricked up until I leaned forward and her ears flattened again. *Wow! Her ears are telling me she's going to act up.*

Over the next few days I became aware of her body language and the rippling of her muscles. When she was going to misbehave, her body reacted differently. As I learned her body language, I changed my timing to be proactive. I would rein her in before she chomped down on the bit, and I would ask her to turn, to disengage her powerful hindquarters, before she could buckle down to run out of control. The problem hadn't been that the pony was a monster. Instead it was my lack of knowledge. Eventually Y-Butt taught me how to ride, and I didn't get dumped by her anymore. We finished off the summer the best of friends.

My dream didn't look anything like I'd imagined. Now I'm firmly convinced God appointed that little Shetland pony to be mine for the summer so I would not only learn to ride but also learn the universal keys, which I've used many times since, to achieve my dreams.

I've noticed that oftentimes when I'm pursing my dreams, they come wrapped in unexpected-looking packages (like a monster pony). Right before my breakthrough is when the obstacles loom the largest (whop! double whop!!). It's so easy to blame the obstacle (Y-Butt), but that never helps me move forward. Instead, I have to take my eyes off the obstacle and look for the solution, which usually means making changes within myself, like seeking more wisdom. Most of all, I learned to never, ever quit when I'm pursing a dream God placed in my heart.

Y-Butt turned out to be the gift God gave me and the leg-up to follow the life of my dreams. The following year for Christmas my parents gave me my very own horse. After college I worked from the saddle for fifteen years, leading guests on horseback trips over the craggy Rocky Mountain trails in the Bob Marshall Wilderness of Montana.

Then God led me down an unexpected path—to an even bigger and more fulfilling dream. Now I love sharing my passion for horses through the books I write.

Ponyfoot

Alison Hodgson

My children and I have not always had good experiences at fairs and carnivals. Actually, we've never had a good experience. Other women might have let this keep them away, but I should tell you, I am not "other women." And that is pretty much all I have for a defense of why, when our annual community fair rolled around again, I thought it would be a good idea to take my three children—Christopher, Lydia, and Eden, who were ten, eight, and three years old. Well, perhaps I considered it a challenge to be met, a sort of mountain to climb.

The fact that the last time we tried to have fun at this fair, five years previous, our adventure ended with an emergency trip to the ophthalmologist did not deter me. My kids were begging to go, and I thought this was our year: we were all older, some of us were wiser, and we could do this. So many people did—you know—be together, have fun, and enjoy festivities.

When we got there we went straight to the rides. Ride is really a misnomer. Attraction might be a better word. We are talking about giant pieces of inflated plastic. There was a bouncing cage, a slide, a whale, and the Velcro run. There was also a rock-climbing wall, a small carousel for the smallest kids, and, excitement of all excitements, pony rides, which began at 11:00.

With us were my sister, Torey, and her three-year-old daughter, Ren, who found the attractions terrorizing. She would wait patiently in line with her cousins and then decline when it was finally her turn. She did enter the whale's mouth only to regurgitate herself within seconds, quavering, "I don't wanna do it!" Torey, a wise woman, decided the craft tent was more their speed. After my kids had exhausted their inflated-plastic options, we met up with Torey and Ren again and headed over to the pony area.

We were a little early, and Torey suggested we get something to eat and return when the pony rides began. That was crazy talk. We were the first ones in line, and I knew we would be fools to give up our place. I put my foot down, and Torey yielded to my greater wisdom. Sure enough, within minutes, people began to line up. By 11:00 the line snaked far into the park.

We were the first in. Christopher and Lydia were directed to the ring of horses while Torey and I placed Ren and Eden on the ponies of their choice. Eden's was a dark-brown pony named Spike. Soon the woman in charge yelled for them to start, and all horses and ponies began plodding in a circle. Walking with Eden, I said all the things a mom says to a small child who is doing something: "Wow! Look at you riding! What a big girl!" You know the drill.

We were moving slowly, but we were under the trees. It felt good to be in the shade and look across the sunny park. Near the ponies, area businesses had set up tents. The one closest belonged to Big Dog Tai Kwon Do School. I was interested in it for the older kids and decided to check it out as soon as we were done with our ride. After that, all that was left of the fair was meandering around the craft area and maybe getting a little something to eat. We had done it! We had come to something intended to be fun for the whole family and the whole family had actually had fun. I was amazed and happy and grateful and relaxed—and then the pony stepped on my foot.

I know, I know, it's not often you get to say that, but I do and did so many times that day: first to Torey, and then to the bewildered women at the Tai Kwon Do tent where I wandered in shock, to the kind ladies at the information booth, to the young man who drove me in a golf cart over to the fire trucks, to the firefighters themselves as one of them iced and bandaged the foot, to my friend who happened by and offered the use of her phone, to my husband, Paul, whom I called to ask for my doctor's number, which I could not remember, to the nurse at the doctor's office, to the doctor my friend ran into and dragged over to check me, to Ronald McDonald as he terrified Ren and Eden while we waited for Torey to get the van, to the woman who checked me into the ER later that day, to the nurse and the doctor and the X-ray tech in the ER.

And then to anyone who happened to notice the colors and size of my foot in the following weeks.

At first I didn't say anything at all. I just crumpled against the pony and groaned loudly. My immediate concerns were things to avoid: yelling bad words, bursting into tears, and attracting any attention.

I can't tell you how much it hurt. I know "pony" sounds so cute and harmless. This is where being pedantic gets one into trouble. A short fat horse stepped on me, technically a pony, but please do not think it was small or light or incapable of inflicting excruciating pain. It was and it did, although I didn't hold Spike personally responsible. I blame the teenage girl who suddenly shouted, "Whoa!" right in his ear, startling him and Eden and me. I was immediately startled again as Spike tried to stop, tripped, stomped on my foot, ground into it to regain his balance, and then stepped off lightly.

After I managed to pull off Eden I staggered across the ring to where Torey was already waiting with the rest of the kids. "The pony stepped on my foot," I whispered.

She covered her mouth with her hand. "Do you need to go to First Aid?"

I was bent over, one hand on my waist, the other on my forehead. "I'm fine," I said.

This is where things get a little fuzzy. Now I know I was in shock and trying to find some way of coping with the astonishing pain other than throwing myself on the ground and sobbing. When I am hurt my impulse is to walk, as though if I keep moving I can escape it.

"I want to check out the Tai Kwon Do tent," I said, and without a backward glance at my three children, began to hobble to it.

Torey watched me as I was still bent over, head nodding, one hand up by my face, the other down by my waist, both alternately pointing and then batting at some invisible assailant.

"You sort of looked like a pecking chicken, an umpire calling a play, and a tottery old lady all rolled into one, but that's not quite it," she told me later.

We'll never know exactly what I resembled as the scattering of our children distracted her from making a perfect study. I was on my own.

When I finally made it to the Big Dog Tai Kwan Do booth, the two women running it jumped to attention, handing me brochures and offering to answer any questions. I stood dumbly. I was struggling to read the brochures and unable to focus; I just stared at them, trying to figure out what had propelled me there. Since becoming a mother, I have often found myself staring blankly, unable to remember why I am wherever I am, so that wasn't a new feeling. But I was realizing that the throbbing pain in my foot, the constriction in my throat, and my inability to remember my name might indicate the need to postpone exploring my martial arts options. The women were still smiling expectantly. An explanation seemed necessary.

"I'm sorry," I said. "A pony just stepped on my foot."

They both gasped and made concerned murmurs. "Do you need anything?" one asked.

I shook my head.

A woman with a baby in a stroller, also visiting the booth, offered me some ibuprofen. I was poised to refuse and then thought better. "That would be great. Thank you."

She whipped out the bottle and handed me a couple of tablets. I took them and stood blinking. She reached down under the stroller and grabbed a bottle of water. "Take this too."

All the refreshments were on the other side of the grassy park, which meant she had gotten this water for herself and then pushed that stroller across the park in the hot sun. I knew how hard it is to push a stroller across grassy and uneven surfaces. For her to give me, a complete stranger, this water that would cost her at least one more trek across the park seemed an extraordinary sacrifice. I was on the verge of tears. In the past bottles of water had been given out free. Good thing I didn't know it also cost her a dollar. Had I known, I am sure I would have refused to take it and started crying in earnest.

Torey, who had gathered all the children, came up as I was thanking my benefactress. I swallowed the Advil as we walked away from the tent. "She gave me Advil and a *bottle of water*!" I said, my voice breaking. "Wasn't that *kiiind*?"

Torey stopped and touched my elbow. "Are you okay?"

I looked at her, amazed. "I got stepped on by a *pooooony*!" This ended in a high-pitched squeal.

"I know! But you were heading off to the Big Dog, leaving me to chase the kids . . ." She paused. This was the moment she realized she was dealing with a lunatic. "You need to go to First Aid. I'll take the kids to the petting zoo. You meet us there when you're finished."

And so I did. Later that day, reclining on a bed in the ER, my husband, Paul, in a chair beside me, I quietly told him my adventures at the carnival.

"I think I acted like such a nut because I was in shock and all my energy was going to holding back tears. Which doesn't make sense since you know what an emotional girl I am." He does; I rarely resist crying. To me, it's just a part of life, a sort of emotional sneeze. My philosophy for crying and sneezing in public is the same: try to be discreet and grab a tissue. There's no need to be embarrassed or ashamed. But when I thought about it, I realized every time I've been hurt physically I have resisted any response and tried to stay calm and ignore the pain. I couldn't understand the distinction I made between physical and emotional pain.

And then I thought of my father's angry voice, saying what he always said when one of his children got hurt enough to cry. "Okay, okay, tuck it in!"

Tuck it in. And we would, because no pain was bigger than our dad's authority.

My siblings and I have talked about how that shaped us. As adults we can see the validity in trying to calm a child, and yet we all got the message that our tearful response to our pain and fears was invalid.

Because I am such an emotional woman, I thought I had eluded "tuck it in," but it was clearly still driving me, at least when it came to physical pain. I, who will calmly wipe away tears prompted by a sad thought, would have rather died than cry when I got stepped on by a stinking pony. In the shock of the pain I thought if I just kept moving, played it cool, and pretended I was okay, I would be.

And it wasn't just me. Sitting in the ER, separated from the other patients by only curtains, every conversation was clearly heard. Person after person, before they would accept care, needed to explain to the doctor exactly how long he or she had held out, some for days, before coming in, and then only at the insistence of a family member. So many of us are reluctant to acknowledge our pain and resist asking for help.

The doctor came back with the news that no bones had been broken, and I was released with instructions to take care. We hadn't been home five minutes before one of the children walked up to hug me and bumped my foot. I bit back a scream.

Days passed and it continued to be brushed against, jostled, and stepped on. After a week Torey was giving me a Pilates lesson and grabbed the foot to adjust my posture.

"Ponyfoot!" I shrieked, and a nickname was born.

It's been months now, the bruises are all gone, and my foot rarely hurts, but every once in a while I still feel a shot of pain and my first thought is always thankfulness that I went to the hospital, because I know everything is fine. The pain is simply a reminder of the ponyfoot wound, and its decreasing frequency a sign of healing.

A Zorse Is a Zorse, of Course, of Course. . . .

The equine animal family includes horses, donkeys, and zebras—as well as the hybrids of them all, such as mules and zorses. Yes, zorses. A zorse—you guessed it—is a cross between a horse and a zebra. Apparently they do fall in love from time to time . . .

Soul Therapy

Pamela S. Thibodeaux

I've always loved horses. One of my earliest memories is being held up by one parent while led around on horseback by the other. Thus began my love of these magnificent creatures. As a girl I devoured stories and books about horses. *Misty of Chincoteague*, Walter Farley's *Black Stallion* series, and of course the classic *Black Beauty* were among my favorites. I read voraciously and dreamed of having a horse of my own.

That day finally came. Stormy, a rich red roan with a lightning stripe down his face, was my first horse. My friend with whom I'd ridden was moving, and the horse was for sale. I'll never forget the day I came home from school to find him in my backyard, or the many times we rode, bareback, my hands wrapped in his mane, my legs tight around his girth. We'd fly, and my dreams soared with each pound of hooves on the ground.

Fast-forward through the years, and horses were a pretty regular part of my life. If I didn't own one, my cousins or friends did, and riding was the most exhilarating thing in my life. On Smokey, a beautiful dark bay with a black mane, tail, and legs, I learned to ride with a saddle, round barrels, and jump ditches. When I was a teen, my uncle owned quarter horses, and I helped cool them down after racing on weekends. I dreamed of becoming a jockey. Then along came Honey, a filly who had been abused and was so skittish we had to approach her with caution. Working with her taught me so much about the tender soul these gentle giants have. By the time I sold her, we'd broken her to a halter, then a bridle. First we rode her bareback, but within a few months, she would be ready for the saddle.

As I matured, my dream of being a jockey lost out to the dream of being a wife and mother. Marriage and babies took the place of horses in my world, but over the years I rode as often as I could.

Then came the worst time of my life. My husband passed away. To say I was lost is an understatement. Nothing made sense anymore. At a time in our lives when the children were all grown and we looked forward to enjoying our time together with grandchildren, he was gone. My job, which had always been a drag, became unbearable, and I felt as though my life was a rut with no meaning or purpose. As someone who suffered "situation induced" depression at various times in my life, I became more and more aware of my feelings, needs, and desires in hopes of avoiding that dark place.

In desperate need of change, I quit my job. I thought if I put as much passion into my writing as I had into my marriage, my career would jump to the next level. I had no idea it would be quite some time before I was emotionally capable of doing any real writing. I couldn't focus or control my thoughts or emotions to write my normal genre of inspirational romance. How could I write romance when the love of my life was gone and I was so cold and empty inside?

While praying about what to do and where to go, one thought emerged and reverberated through my soul. . . . *If only I could be around horses.* I knew horses had a way of healing the heart and soul. I knew just as I'd helped heal the broken spirit of Honey, these wonderful animals would have the ability to do the same for me.

I had left my job at the end of the year. Winter is my least favorite season, and the thought of exercising or grooming horses and mucking stalls in freezing temperatures held little appeal. So I put off contacting the area horse farms and stables. However, I'd registered for a writers retreat to be held at a guest ranch in Bandera, Texas, for the end of April. I looked forward to the warmth of spring and the activities—especially the trail rides—that would be offered during that weekend.

As a child I'd traveled to Bandera with my grandparents when they went to visit a longtime friend of theirs. I fell in love with the area—so much so that I set a whole series of novels there. The memory of that beautiful place in the hill country and the thought of being around horses again filled me with a sense of anticipation and hope that I hadn't felt since before my husband died. What I didn't know was how God would use this experience, and this place, to answer my prayer and fulfill the desire of my heart.

The minute I turned off Hwy 1604 onto Hwy 16N and saw the sign, "Bandera 32 miles," I felt as though the whole world lifted off my shoulders. Exhilarating as that was, the sentiment was nothing compared to what grabbed hold of me driving through the gate of the Silver Spur Guest Ranch.

So powerful was the sensation of coming home. Add to that a weekend filled with laughter, music, dancing, horses, and people I'd known only through the internet, plus the love and support, awesome beauty of the Texas Hill Country, and the lure of life itself . . . Well, to say I did not want to leave when the retreat ended is an understatement. Even today I can close my eyes and still feel the sense of desperation, of longing for purpose and a reason to live I harbored back then.

I cried all the way back to my home in Louisiana and for several days afterward. The retreat confirmed one truth in my heart and mind: I had no idea what I wanted to do, but I knew I did *not* want to stay in my house anymore. The depression I consciously sought to avoid crept closer, threatening to take over.

While on the trail rides I had talked with the wranglers and learned that the ranch manager often hired summer help. The idea of being on horseback in those lovely hills on a regular basis pushed me into applying for a position. Then the fears set in . . . What if they didn't hire me? What would I do with my house if they did? I couldn't leave it unattended for half the year. And what about my dog?

But God had all the details covered. A friend in need of a home came to live with me and take care of my dog, and I got the job beginning June 1. For some reason during that first year after my husband's death, the three-month marks hit me hardest, and May was no different. So much to do, so many events to attend . . . culminating with the memorial service during National Law Enforcement Week when he was honored. Only the thought of leaving at the end of the month kept me hanging on and the despair at bay.

The next six months became the best medicine my grieving heart could have taken. I rode almost daily. I helped saddle or unsaddle when I could. I swam, walked, hiked, and found a peace of mind and solace of soul I never dreamed possible. Riding horses set me free in a way nothing I'd done before had—or has since. My heart began to mend, my soul to heal, and my creativity to return.

I continue to work at the Silver Spur Guest Ranch on occasion, and I ride every chance I get. I still grieve the loss of my husband, but I've been able to move forward. Looking back at how fragile my emotional state was, I find it amazing how God perfectly orchestrated every aspect of this experience of being around horses in a place that had touched me so deeply as a child. There's not a doubt in my mind that being on this ranch, in that season, saved my life.

My North Dakota Horses

Shirley Zeller

I grew up in a remote area of North Dakota during the 1940s and 1950s. I lived on a nineteen-hundred-acre farm with my mother and my stepdad, Meade, who became very much a father to me. My siblings were older and gone most of my growing up years.

Meade was a cowboy who worked the farm, the horses, and the land. We had many horses, and we used them for everything—for work, for pleasure, for survival of the other animals, and even for getting us to school. We bought, broke, and sold horses on a regular basis, and we were well known in the area for this. On Sunday afternoons cowboys, cowgirls, and interested observers enjoyed coming to our place to watch us break and train horses. We'd come home from church, have dinner with anyone who showed up, then get ready for the rodeo. Even as a kid I helped round up and ready the horses for action, and it was always a lively time. The money we got from this business paid my college tuition down the road.

Since we had no close neighbors, horses were my best friends. I was around nine years old when I got my first pony, a beautiful strawberry roan, part Shetland. Her name was Goldie, and she was a beauty. I rode her everywhere. She loved to race. If we were in a rodeo barrel race or any other race, she would strive to be the fastest—and usually was. Cars seldom came by our place, but when one did, she would try to outrun it. She loved to get out on the prairie and run as fast as she could. I loved it too and would urge her on.

Goldie was a young bride, and when her first baby came, she didn't know how to take care of it. She shunned it and wouldn't feed it. My stepdad was in love with his horses, and when he discovered Goldie's dilemma, he brought the baby indoors. Early in the morning, Meade carried the little filly upstairs to my bedroom, and I woke to a snuggly, velvety, cold, baby-horse nose. I named her Sunshine because, at that point, she was the sunshine of my life.

Sunshine was a beautiful sorrel filly, and we became the best of friends. She was only about two and a half feet tall. I fed her with a baby bottle and led her around the yard. She was born near the Fourth of July, and there was always a big parade in the small town near us, so I decided Sunshine and I would be in the parade. She was so pretty with her red, white, and blue collar and a little halter, and she followed me. I carried a full baby bottle of milk to coax her along through the crowd, and we marched proudly up the street. She was, of course, the hit of the parade.

In the middle of winter, Goldie had another filly. That baby was chased by one of the bigger horses in the barn, and she fell and hurt her foot. In the cold weather, the end of her foot was frozen. My horse-loving stepdad doctored her until the frozen part of her foot fell off. Then Meade made her a leather shoe that came up around her ankle so she could walk and run normally. As she grew, Meade made the shoe bigger. And it worked.

Goldie continued to have a foal about every year, and eventually Sunshine joined the ranks of motherhood too. But Goldie and Sunshine remained what could now be called my BFFs (Best Friends Forever). They were not the only horses I rode and loved, but they were the only ones who were mine.

All our horses were named, and we knew all their names. I'm not sure the horses knew their names, but it seemed like they did. There was Bluebell, my mother's horse, who would blow up her belly when we put the saddle on her, and then partway on a ride she would exhale. The saddle would slide forward, and my mother would go over Bluebell's head and onto the ground. There was Smokey, one of Goldie's offspring, who was a gentle, nicely trained horse until we sold him to someone who didn't treat him well. They brought him back and said he wasn't any good, but he went right back to his gentle self after being back in our "fold."

I often rode an older horse named Ginger—a big black horse with a white face and one white foot. He was our utility horse but also a good buddy to me. He's the one I would ride to get the cows for milking or herd the cattle to the well for drinking or whatever chore we needed to do. If I was away from the farm and dropped the reins, though, Ginger would run to the barn as fast as he could. That was his favorite place.

Midnight was a fat, all-black Shetland pony. He was a little mean sometimes, so I had to let him know who was boss. If he was tired of being ridden around the farm—and he didn't ride very fast or very far—he would go to the low-hanging tree that was just the right height for him to get under with no one on his back.

Every day my job was to get the daily mail. The mailbox was a mile and a half from our farm, so I would often test to see how long it would take to get to the mailbox on horseback. Or I might simply take my time and enjoy the ride. In my free time, I would jump on my horse and ride—fast, slow, trot, gallop—whatever I felt like at the moment.

My absolute favorite thing to do was ride out to the pasture, loosen the reins for my horse to graze, lie back on its back, watch the clouds, and sing. I'm pretty sure my horses were tone-deaf, so the singing didn't matter—and I really enjoyed it. My little dog, Patsy, would run along with us, sometimes chasing a fox into the fox den. It was her favorite thing to do, and she was just about their size. Or she would lie down and keep me company.

> "When confronted with the healing presence of an animal, I am warmed by a sense of hope for the world."
>
> CASEY CARPENTER

In the very coldest, snowiest winters, the well in our big cattle pasture would freeze. We had over a hundred animals, and they all needed water. Meade and I would bundle ourselves, saddle a couple of horses, and head for the pasture a mile from home. There we'd open gates and herd the cattle for their daily water to an open spring that never froze. We'd keep them together and watch over them until all were satisfied, then we'd drive them back to the pasture, where we'd spread hay for them to eat. Our horses were good herders, and our many dogs would keep all the cattle in line.

In those winters, attending a one-room school a mile and a half from home could be a challenge. My mom was the school-teacher, so we had to go even in bad weather. We had to arrive at the schoolhouse early to get the heat going for the other students before they arrived. Meade would hitch one of the big, beautiful Percherons to a hay sleigh, cover us with a heavy horsehide blanket, and away we would go. At the end of the day, Meade would return to take us home.

When that school closed, I attended another school three and a half miles away. In good weather, I would pedal my bike there or ride my big white horse. Whitey was a registered Arabian. One day Whitey bucked me off on the way home from school, but she stood and waited for me to get back on. At home I told our hired man about her behavior, and he said, "Oh, she doesn't buck." When he got on to take care of Whitey, she promptly bucked him off too.

The next day when I went to saddle Whitey to ride to school, she wasn't where she should be. After we located her, we found her with her new baby. What a surprise! Whitey was supposed to have a registered foal, but her baby was a mule. Obviously, I had to ride a different horse that day. We named the mule Jenny, and pretty soon Jenny followed Whitey and me every-where we went.

In the winter when the road was impassable for anything but the horses, early Monday morning Meade would bring my horse, ready to go, to our front door. I would be dressed for blizzard weather. We rode three miles to a neighbor's house where I would stay all week and go to school with them. We would travel to the school from their house with a horse and sleigh wagon. This is how I got my education.

Eventually I left the farm for college, where I met the man I would marry. Today we live in Michigan. I have saved many personal mementos from my cowgirl childhood, and I display them in my Michigan home as a testament to our North Dakota farm and all my horse friends. I show guests a framed photo of my beloved stepdad, Meade, wearing his cowboy clothes, including chaps and a hat. I love telling people he did not dress this way for the picture. That's the way he always dressed, because he was an authentic cowboy who gave me a wonderful childhood as a cowgirl with the best of friends—horses.

Swimming with Cheetah

Lonnie Hull DuPont

At age six I developed a problem with anxiety, and it changed me. It caused me to have thoughts and feelings my young mind didn't understand and could not describe. Since I grew up in a quiet household where talking wasn't encouraged, I kept my worries to myself for the most part. One way I coped with anxious feelings was to be around animals. They were my friends and confidantes, and I felt soothed and grounded in their presence.

When I was eleven and my sister was fourteen, we got our first horse, a handsome palomino gelding named Pal. Later on, along came Sundy Sue Burgundy, a gorgeous Thoroughbred who stayed with us for only a short time because she was so mean; Lady and Honey, two good-natured pony mares (Honey was mine); and Shadow, the adorable, goofy colt born to Lady on our stepfather's birthday.

I have many good memories of the horses. I loved watching them move. I loved their brown eyes and long lashes, especially Honey's blonde lashes. I remember liking to watch the steam pump from their flared nostrils on cold mornings as they waited for their grain. We would celebrate their birthdays by feeding them huge carrots—and then we humans would feed ourselves my mother's homemade carrot cake. I would hear Pal whinny my sister awake outside her bedroom window every morning, and one day he whinnied me awake first to sound the news that Lady had given birth in the tree line. Nervous Uncle Pal wanted the humans up and moving.

Pal was the horse we saddled and rode Western style. He didn't always like to be saddled, but I discovered a secret weapon to get him to comply when I wanted to ride: grab my sweet-natured gray cat, Fluffy, and take her into the field. For some reason, Pal was crazy for this cat. All I had to do was walk to the middle of the field with the cat draped on my shoulder and sing out, "Oh Paaaal . . . look what I have . . ."

Pal would slowly approach, his head bobbing up and down with happy curiosity. He'd nuzzle the cat with his big soft nose. As Fluffy purred on my shoulder, the horse simply followed the cat and me into the barn. I'd plop the purring cat into the manger, where Pal continued to nuzzle her, seemingly oblivious to my presence, and then I saddled him with ease. Sometimes my sister would lead Pal to the front yard to graze where the grass was especially green, and I'd place Fluffy on his back. She'd stretch and purr, and the horse seemed blissed by her presence as he grazed. Every now and then, he'd reach around and try to nuzzle her, and she'd bat at his nose, claws in.

One aspect of my childhood anxiety was insomnia. The nights were long for me. My bedtime was the one thing my parents actually negotiated with me, making a deal that if I'd take a nap (which for me meant lying awake on my bed in the middle of the day), I could stay up later at night. Long after my older sister went to bed, I would still be allowed up. When finally I went to my room at the agreed-upon time, I'd lie awake in the dark. I'd hear my parents watching the eleven o'clock news on television, hear them going to their bedroom, hear my stepfather snoring. And I'd lie awake some more.

In my world of worry, however, there were two things I had an almost unnatural lack of fear of—water and animals. We always had pets in addition to the horses—a rabbit, a stray rooster, many cats and dogs. We lived in the country, and the neighbor's cows would gather at the fence that bordered our properties and listen to me sing to them. The presence of animals in the wild was also stabilizing for me when I was outdoors—songbirds, deer, rabbits, an occasional fox or turtle—these creatures distracted me by day.

At night the jingle of the family dog's tags was a comfort as he wandered around. Sometimes he slept on the rug next to my bed while my hand dangled over his head. My cats slept at the foot of my bed. On hot summer nights I'd prop my pillow on the sill of an open window next to my bed, and I'd listen to the bullfrogs in the swamp, the owls, the neighbor's collie barking at the moon, the rustling of creatures under my window, creatures unknown yet not feared. I'd hear deer tromp through the swamp water. I'd watch the shadows of the horses in the orchard behind the house. Sometimes they were joined by the deer, and the shadowy beasts moved quietly around each other in the grass. I would pray about what was making me anxious as I watched and listened to the animals, sometimes half the night, and it soothed my worries.

Shortly after we got Pal, I attended a ranch camp to learn to ride horses. My sister had gone there the year before me and had had a wonderful time, but she and I were very different children. I agreed to go with a mixture of hopes and dread. But I was not a child who should have been away from home for an entire month with strangers. I was homesick to the point of being physically ill most of the time.

In spite of the homesickness, I managed to have good times at the ranch. I can still recall the sweet, heavy smell of the pines outside the window where I bunked. Around campfires at night, we sang folk songs, accompanied by college student counselors playing guitars. Like at home, I dealt with my feelings by seeking out the animals. I especially enjoyed playing with the ranch's donkeys, trying to ride them or to get them to move at all; they truly were stubborn. And we were always around plenty of horses.

I especially liked the Chippewa River, which ran through the ranch. This river wound its ninety or so miles through Central Michigan, and at the ranch, it was lined by green leafy trees. One of the ranchers at the time told me the water was fast enough and clean enough to drink. I loved being in that river, canoeing or floating on my back or crossing it on horseback, watching the shores for any wildlife to show itself in the brush. Taking a dip in that clean, chilly water was a great way to cool off after morning riding, and I taught myself to swim there. Although these were the days of more casual handling of children, it's still hard to believe that at age eleven I was often in the water alone, swimming in a river with no adults nearby. But that was the case. I still sometimes have vivid dreams of that lovely green river.

Each camper was given a horse to ride for the month, and mine was a big patient mare named Cheetah. She was chocolate brown with wide patches of white and a broad back. I was told she was twenty-four years old, and she was just what I needed—an older, gentle beast who helped me to become a decent rider. The first time we cantered bareback, I did everything wrong and slid right off her. I dropped to the ground with a thud, and Cheetah simply stopped and waited. Another time I hadn't cinched my saddle tight enough, and as we trotted, it bounced to the side and slid under the horse's belly, dumping me in the process. That could have been especially dangerous given the stirrups, but again, Cheetah stopped and waited. She certainly showed this child some equine grace.

During that month we campers had an occasional overnight sleep-out. We rode our horses to a faraway field, where we camped under the stars. Since even at the ranch I had trouble sleeping, I would lie awake on my bedroll and watch in the distance the ranch's herds of horses moving around in starlight. It reminded me of being home in my open window at night, watching the shadows of our few horses.

One day we campers rode bareback while in our bathing suits and were told we were going to cross the river on our horses. This is something we often did through shallow spots, saddled. But on this day, we crossed the river at a place I'd never been. I knew from swimming that the water could be deep down the center, but I didn't realize how deep this was going to be.

Cheetah lumbered down the grassy embankment as I hung on to her mane. She stepped into the water and splashed it all over me. As she walked in deeper, it surprised me that the water rose around my waist. Deeper still we went, until I felt her pick up her hooves and begin to swim. Soon only her head and part of her neck were above water, and her movements were smooth and seamless. I nervously hung on to her mane and eventually floated in the water straight out over her submerged back.

Once I knew this was how it was supposed to be—that a horse really could swim and I could hang on to her and enjoy the water I loved—I relaxed. In fact, I felt completely at peace. It almost felt like I was flying as Cheetah and I moved together through the cool river. Even at that young age, I knew I was lucky to be swimming with this huge animal. We swam together only a few times that August, but those serve as some of my happiest memories of childhood.

When I returned home, I was a capable rider, though it would always be my sister who was more involved with the horses. By the time I was in high school, only Pal remained with us, and when my sister went to college, she reluctantly sold him. A few years later she married a man who had a construction company that worked with heavy, earth-moving equipment. A year or so into their marriage, my sister learned that she could buy Pal back—and so she did. He lived out his years with my sister, and when he died, my brother-in-law used his heavy equipment to bury Pal on their property.

My sister went on to have other horses. I never had another horse, though I became more involved with animals in general, both with pets and in the wild. My anxiety continued into my adult years. I never told anyone about it until I was well into middle age, and only then was I able to understand what it was and how to handle it. I still find living with animals to be a good way of self-medicating, and when my anxiety hits particularly hard, I have learned many coping mechanisms. One is to pull up certain scenes and sounds from my life that my mind can use for calming—for example, an experience of puppies climbing all over me; stroking Fluffy while she purrs on Pal's back; brushing the thick winter coat of my pony Honey. I am grateful for these good memories. Through the years, I've added others: sailing on the Mediterranean on a thirty-foot boat; replaying in my mind a certain hymn from church I find particularly calming; watching my brother-in-law's cattle line up and, one by one, greet a newborn calf in the corral.

But my favorite go-to memory for quelling my anxiety is remembering swimming with Cheetah. In my mind I see that green river lined by leafy trees. I can feel the clean water on my skin, the August sun over my head, the power of that huge mare as she lifts her hooves and swims, and the sense of freedom from worries I feel while floating over her. Those worries seem to sink into the deep Chippewa River for a while. And I am calm.

Acknowledgments

Many thanks to my animal-loving, award-winning, ever-patient editor, Dr. Vicki Crumpton, who first caught and represented the vision for a book of horse stories. Thanks to those committee members at Revell, a division of Baker Publishing Group, who shared their love of horses—and sometimes their dreams of having them—as they made decisions about this book. Thanks to the gifted staff members in the editorial, marketing, publicity, sales, and art departments at Revell for their creativity and hard work. And special thanks to the generous writers in this book, who trusted us with their stories.

Notes

1. Vicky Moon, *The Private Passion of Jackie Kennedy Onassis: Portrait of a Rider* (New York: Harper Design, 2005), 152.

2. Melissa Sovey-Nelson, *If I Had a Horse How Different Life Would Be* (Minocqua, WI: Willow Creek Press, 2004), 11.

3. Ibid, 90.

4. Moon, *The Private Passion of Jackie Kennedy Onassis*, 68, 82, 98, 102.

5. Thomas Merton, "Conscience, Freedom, and Prayer," *No Man Is an Island* (Boston: Shambhala Publications, 2005), 35.

6. 2 Timothy 1:7 KJV.

7. Philippians 4:13 NLT.

8. Luke 6:31.

9. Not her real name.

Contributors

Donna Acton is a licensed veterinary technician who has worked in veterinary hospitals for over three decades. As the daughter of a veterinarian, she has had a lifelong interest in helping pets and the people they live with. Her professional focus now is behavior training for dogs and cats.

Long-time English professor at Cornerstone University **Cynthia Beach** also serves as a writing and creativity coach through her organization Soul Seasons (SoulSeasons.org). She cofounded the Breathe Christian Writers Conference in Grand Rapids, Michigan. Her novel manuscript, *The Seduction of Pastor Goodman*, is under consideration for publication.

Catherine Ulrich Brakefield has numerous short stories in print and is the author of two history books and two historical romances, the most recent novel titled *Wilted Dandelions*. She and her husband, Edward, have two fabulous children and three grandchildren. Meet her horses at www.facebook.com/Catherine UlrichBrakefield and www.CatherineUlrichBrakefield.com.

With a passion to help writers get their words into print, **Mary Busha** has worn many hats in the publishing world over the past thirty-five years, and she continues to coach writers, edit manuscripts, and offer workshops. Wife, mother, and grandmother, Mary makes her home in Jackson, Michigan, with her husband, Bob. She is also the happy owner of Noah, her marbled tabby cat. Mary can be contacted at yourtimetowrite@gmail.com.

Robert W. Busha, also known as "Dr. Bob," is a life coach, a full-time encourager, and a prolific author of primarily commercial nonfiction and curriculum materials. He's also an adjunct professor in the MBA program for Spring Arbor University's Gainey School of Business. Bob is the author/editor of *Take Five*, a three-book devotional series for men, and *Minute Master: Investing Wisely Your Most Valuable God-given Asset—The Rest of Your Life!* Since 1993 Bob and his wife, Mary, have served as missionaries within the continental United States, working with church, parachurch, and community leadership teams.

Sarah Dowlearn is a freelance writer and poet living in the San Francisco Bay Area. When she's not scribbling rhymes or discovering new fonts, she uses her degree in equine science to manage a therapeutic riding program for children with special needs. Sarah has been published in *Brass* magazine, and she blogs about horses, hobbies, and issues relevant to young adults. Learn more at www.SarahDowlearn.com.

Lonnie Hull DuPont is a book editor, award-winning poet, and writer of nonfiction who lives with her husband and their cats in her hometown in Southeastern Michigan.

In addition to being an avid horse lover and a fan/owner of German Shepherds, **Wanda Dyson** is the critically acclaimed author of eight "high-octane" suspense novels and the coauthor with Tina Zahn of *Why I Jumped*. She currently lives in North Carolina, working on her next novel. For more information on Wanda's books, you can visit her website at www.WandaDyson .com.

Gwen Ellis and her daughter, Wendy Weising, run an editorial and writing service called Seaside Creative Services. Gwen is the author of more than twenty-seven books, including the best-selling *Read and Share Bible*. She lives in Old Hickory, Tennessee.

Suzanne Woods Fisher is a best-selling, award-winning author of fiction and nonfiction books about the Old Order Amish for Revell, a division of Baker Publishing Group. One of her favorite hobbies is to raise puppies for Guide Dogs for the Blind. You can find Suzanne online at www.suzannewoodsfisher.com.

Susy Flory grew up on the back of a quarter horse in Northern California. The author or coauthor of nine books, including the *New York Times* bestseller *Thunder Dog*, Susy was recently named director of the West Coast Writers Conference. She is a wife and the mom of two grown humans and a goofy retired racehorse named Stetson. She occasionally works up the courage to ride him but needs stairs to get up that high.

Sherri Gallagher generally writes about German Shepherds and canine search and rescue, but she couldn't resist telling the stories of a few of the horses that influenced her life. She has written and had published a teen novel and several short stories;

some are offered free on her website, www.SherriGallagher .com. She is active on Facebook and LinkedIn, where you can touch base and share your own experiences. Currently her agent is working to place Sherri's contemporary romantic suspense novels.

Callie Smith Grant loves animals of all kinds. She is the author of many animal stories, the author of several books for young readers, and the compiler of the anthologies *The Dog Next Door*, *The Cat in the Window*, *The Dog at My Feet*, and *The Cat in My Lap*.

Alison Hodgson is a writer, speaker, and cofounder of Breathe Christian Writers Conference. She is a regular contributor to Houzz.com, and her work has been featured on Her.meneutics, the *Christianity Today* blog for women, Religion News Service, and Forbes.com. Contact her about speaking at alisonhodgson. net. Find her on Facebook at https://www.facebook.com/alison. hodgson.754 and Twitter @HodgsonAlison.

Audrey Leach has worked in the publishing business for over twenty years. When she is not reading books, she is promoting books. And when she is doing neither, she is involved with her local chapter of Friends of the Library. Gardening in her lovely flower beds, however, does make her forget all about books.

Clyde McKaney began studying the violin in the public school system, and while still a high school student he joined the Jackson, Michigan, orchestra in his hometown. He went on to study music at the University of Michigan, Michigan State University, and the Julliard School. Clyde lives in his hometown, where he is the principal violist of the Jackson Symphony, teaches, conducts the Jackson Symphony Orchestra Community String Ensemble, and enjoys training and riding his horse.

Nicole M. Miller is a novelist, blogger, and former rodeo queen. She is the community champion for Buffer (bufferapp.com), a social media management tool. When she's not connecting with the awesome Buffer community, she's riding her horse, Grunnion, or chasing after her fourteen chickens, four ducks, and two dogs. She and her husband live in Portland, Oregon. Connect and read more at nicolemillerbooks.com.

Horses!—a word that has dramatically transformed **Rebecca E. Ondov's** life. From the fifteen years she worked from the saddle in the Bob Marshall Wilderness of Montana, she has corralled her own true-to-life Wild West horse stories (and hair-raising adventures) into her books, *Horse Tales from Heaven* and *Heavenly Horse Sense*, which will inspire you with blazing faith. She loves it when her readers connect with her on Facebook and through her website: http://RebeccaOndov.com. Rebecca invites you to "saddle up and ride with me, through the pages of my books, for an adventure of a lifetime."

Sarah Parshall Perry is the author of *Sand in My Sandwich* and the coauthor of *When the Fairy Dust Settles*. Her stories, articles, and essays have been published in print and online across the country. Sarah received her JD from the University of Virginia School of Law and currently writes for www.Chosen Families, where she uses her sons' autism spectrum diagnoses to encourage families living with disabilities. Sarah also serves as senior fellow at the Family Research Council, where she writes and speaks on education policy and reform. Most of this she does in muck boots.

Katy Pistole is the executive director of Beautiful Brokenness, a horse-themed teaching and discipleship ministry located in Central Virginia. God has used horses to reveal his heart for Katy since she was twelve years old. Today Katy is a wholehearted daughter of the King, award-winning author, speaker, and ordained minister. You can trot over to www.KatyPistole.com or www.BeautifulBrokenness.org to find out more about Katy.

Rachel Anne Ridge is an artist, writer, and owner of two rescue donkeys in Texas. You can find her online at RachelAnne Ridge.com, where she blogs about finding beauty and purpose in unexpected places. She is the author of the book *Flash— The Homeless Donkey Who Taught Me about Life, Faith, and Second Chances.*

Lauraine Snelling is the award-winning author of over seventy novels, including the beloved Red River of the North series. When not writing she can be found, paintbrush in hand, creating flowers and landscapes. She and her husband, Wayne, live in the Tehachapi Mountains in California with their basset, Sir Winston.

Claudia Wolfe St. Clair is an artist and art therapist from Toledo, Ohio. In her early adult life, while living in Virginia, she was a frequent visitor at the stables on Fort Myer. She and her mother, June, attended Black Jack's birthday party every year until his death, delivering his favorite strawberry Jello.

Award-winning author **Pamela S. Thibodeaux** is the cofounder and a lifetime member of Bayou Writers Group in Lake Charles, Louisiana. Multi-published in romantic fiction as well as in creative nonfiction, her writing has been tagged as "Inspirational with an Edge!"™ and reviewed as "steamier and grittier than the typical Christian novel *without* decreasing the message." Website address: http://www.pamelathibodeaux.com. Blog: http://pamswildroseblog.blogspot.com. Facebook: http://facebook.com/pamelasthibodeaux. Twitter: http://twitter.com/psthib @psthib.

Shirley Zeller is retired from BWXT Technologies, where she was assigned to various Department of Energy facilities around the United States. Currently she serves as president of the Board of the Michigan Women's Studies Association and also as chair of the Advisory Board of the Salvation Army in her area. Shirley loves to quilt and do other crafts. In her home, she keeps a designated cowboy room and a designated cowgirl room, each filled with Western pictures and personal memorabilia, including a bridle handmade by her beloved stepfather for her mother's horse and a "Drink Root Beer" cowgirl clock.

A wagging tail. A goofy, floppy-tongued smile.
An excited bark when your keys jingle in the door.

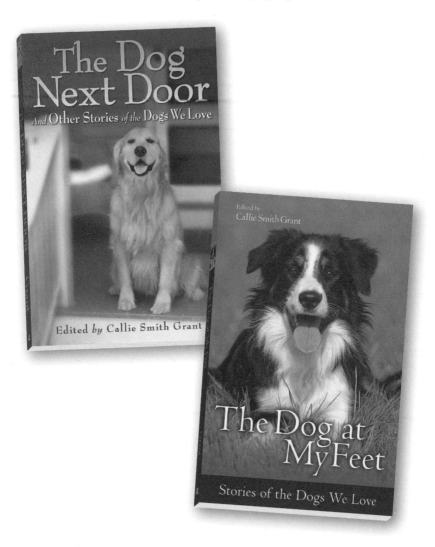

Enjoy these heartwarming collections of true dog stories!

A playful bat of a string. A bored yawn.
A tender purr at the touch of your hand.

Enjoy these delightful collections of true cat stories!

Sometimes you seek out love.
And sometimes it broadsides you.

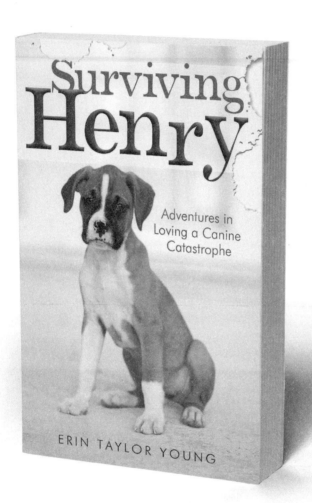